Shake Your Booty:
How to Teach Belly Dance for Fun and Profit

TAAJ

Copyright © 2013 TAAJ

All rights reserved.

ISBN: 0974120820
ISBN-13: 978-0974120829

DEDICATION

To wild dingoes in dark alleys, early morning dirty monkeys, dining *insha'allah* fresco, Afrosenses, cathouses, men in black, sequins in the sand, death defying taxi rides, falling asleep to the call of the the *muezzin*, and everyone who understands what any of that means.

CONTENTS

	Acknowledgments	i
1	Introduction	1
2	Before the Class	5
3	Teaching Methods	31
4	Body Mechanics	55
5	Music Theory for Dancers	73
6	Middle Eastern Rhythms	87
7	Finger Cymbals	97
8	Musicality	105
9	Choreography	117
10	Improvisation	131

ACKNOWLEDGMENTS

This book would not be possible were it not for my students of 2001- 2007. Magic happened then that brought together people who were eager to learn and an instructor who was hungry to teach. The more they grew, the more inspired I was to lead them to the next achievement. We pushed each other to go further than we could ever dream of going alone. And what an enchanted journey it was.

I'd also like to acknowledge the people who acted as guinea pigs to help me to test the Belly Dance Trainer Method. It took a lot of time and dedication to see that process through. I'm so proud of you. Your feedback was invaluable.

Thank-you Memie Ayat, Kalaa, Rachel, Charlotte Aaberg, Jasmin, Najla, Ruhiyyih, Shalah, Inaras, Brianna, Sorsha, Andrea, Chelsea, Sharon, Vasiliki, Sabah, Gamilla, Zuleika, Nadira, Emiko and so many others. Because of you, this book is possible.

1 INTRODUCTION

The Belly Dance Trainer (BDT) Method is a holistic system for teaching belly dance. When you see this learning and teaching style in motion, you will recognize it. The dance will be visually pleasing, it will reflect the music, touch your emotions, and make sense. If you asked the dancer how and why those things occur, she may say that learning the BDT way is not just a body building experience, but also a mind building one.

Outside of the belly dance world, teaching dance conceptually is not new. Unfortunately I had no teachers like that within belly dance. All that was available to me, and in fact all I gave to my students when I started teaching, was steps, combinations, and choreographies. When you teach steps, combinations, and choreographies, it is like giving your students words, sentences, and books to copy. Armed with those, they can give you back someone else's story. They may also be able to give you a passable story of their own. However, to become a true artist with elegance, creativity, innovation, and the ability to replicate that same success in a different way requires more than those basic elements.

If you are to create true dancers, you need to understand ALL the elements of dance, how they fit together, why they fit together, what rules make them work together, and how and when to deviate from the rules to create certain effects. It is this underlying structure that makes great dance possible and solid results predictable.

When I began grooming students for competition, creating proficient dancers with these abilities became my goal. I share what I learned with you now so that you can do the same.

As this is a new way of thinking for most belly dancers, let me help to explain it by telling you what it's not.

This method is not about:

• *Movement vocabulary with specific names that is done in a particular way.* Although it helps to have a common vocabulary, dancers who have learned other names for movements can continue to use those words. There are many variations of movement. Because the Belly Dance Trainer Method is not restricted to one way of teaching movement, the variety of things you can do within the method are endless. Rest assured, fabulous teachers can use any vocabulary.

• *Instruction on a particular belly dance style.* The techniques taught within the method can be used to learn and teach any style.

• *Choreography.* Although choreography construction is taught and choreographies are used to illustrate concepts, choreography is only one tool used in the method.

The Belly Dance Trainer Method is:

• *A western way of teaching an eastern topic.* It utilizes concepts that build upon each other, so that the student has a comprehensive view of movement and music as seen through Middle Eastern culture.

- *A self-paced way of learning.* You aren't expected to master the concepts immediately. It takes time for them to soak in and deepen. The concepts overlap, so they are constantly reinforced. Eventually the light *will* come on and understanding will happen.

- *Respectful of your individuality.* It is not about creating Taaj clones. Each dancer can develop her own style and her own personality. Each teacher has a lot of freedom to personalize the method.

- *A teaching method as well as a learning method.* The method will improve your dancing as it teaches you how to teach.

Why Learn to Teach The Belly Dance Trainer Way?

The method is comprehensive. It attacks issues such as movement, musicality, dance construction, stage presence, and improvisation head on so that development isn't haphazard or incidental. The objective framework helps students become more comfortable in self-correction. Consequently, they tend to grow faster. Students are more confident in their abilities, because there is a way to measure their progress. Better students translate into a more successful business.

What Other Benefits Are There?

- *You'll get more business.* My method makes it easy to create winners and pros. If you desire, soon you will have a display case full of trophies that will attest to *your* record of creating high quality dancers.

- *You'll work smarter, not harder.* I have done most of the work for you, so you'll spend less time lesson planning and figuring out how to help students *get* it.

- *You'll make more money with less effort.* Dance studios profit by attracting and retaining students. With a proven method and strong brand behind you, students will stay because they are learning. This allows you to spend less time and money marketing, advertising, and doing public relations to get new business in the door.

* *You will feel more confident about what you are doing.* The methods within this book are tried and true. You won't have to worry about random results anymore. Instead, you can use these techniques as a baseline to reach your business goals.

How to Improve the Learning Process

Keep a notebook. As you work on each section, write notes about what worked and what didn't. When repeating a lesson, workshop, or session, keep the things that worked. Use your own written feedback to change the things that didn't work. Refer back to your notes when needed to measure your progress and remind yourself to continue using the material taught in previous chapters. Your notes are your best tool for creating reliable habits and dynamic tools.

Take your time. The vast majority of the material is conceptual. It takes a while for concepts to sink in. When you fully explore and understand a concept, you can take it out of context and apply it elsewhere. That is the beauty of learning *ideas* rather than steps, combinations, and choreographies. It expands your learning by leaps and bounds, rather than giving you one piece of information at a time. So don't race through the material. Depth of understanding is much more valuable than speed. People who work with the material for a while tend to get better results, both in the short term and the long term, than those who race through.

This material was originally part of the BDT certification program. The original assessments are included. Be sure to read the assessment criteria. This reiterates what the lesson was all about. Use the assessments. Give yourself an honest appraisal of how you and your students did. If it is possible, get a third party to assess your teaching skills. A second set of eyes is invaluable.

Use the assessment feedback to make your work stronger. If you find yourself getting angry or feeling like a failure, take a break and come back to it when you can be more objective. Part of the reason for feedback is to teach you how to give it. An effective teacher doesn't just tell her students, "You look great" and move on. You have to be able to balance praise with constructive criticism. Praise doesn't make people better. Pointing out what could be better and then showing them how to get there does.

Putting your work out there for critique takes a lot of courage. No one wants to feel like they aren't doing a good job, and that is not what this is about. It's about learning to accept feedback, using it to be better, and learning how to deal with it.

Sometimes feedback is meaningless! The only way to really know if you have something you can use or not is to listen to a lot of feedback so that you have a basis for comparison. Assess it objectively. Discern what is opinion, and therefore subjective, and what is objective. "Your body line is falling apart" is a pretty objective observation. Either it is or it isn't. "Your make-up is too gaudy" is subjective. Sometimes it will be worthwhile and other times you can disregard it.

Good critique is a gift. It's a gift to you, and it's a gift you give your students. In my opinion, it's the most worthwhile piece of this program. I believe that if you learn to use it wisely, you will have a huge edge over any competitors because there are too many teachers who can't or won't give constructive feedback. Critique is not about you personally. It's about the work, how effective it is, and how it can be better.

Good luck to you. You have embarked on a journey that will bring you lots of personal fulfillment and better-trained students if you use it effectively. It may not always be easy. If your experience is anything like mine, and that of the others who have tested this program, it will be incredibly rewarding.

Should you wish to have me critique your work, that service is available for a fee. Email me at Taaj@rocketmail.com or see my website at www.thebellydancetrainer.com to find out more. Passing all nine chapters will certify you in my method.

If you would like more help in using these principles, please obtain my book <u>Beyond Moves, Combos, and Choreography</u>. It contains eighty-two lesson plans, games, and exercises that you can use in your classes to build strong skills.

2 BEFORE THE CLASS

Goal: Students will be able to create a logical outline for a class, including an assessment tool.

Objectives:
- Students will be able to create goals for their class.
- Students will be able to define objectives for their class.
- Students will be able to write a course description.
- Students will create a lesson plan that shows progress toward the objectives of the class, fits the skill level of the students within the class, can be completed within the time frame allowed, and have an objective way of measuring whether the objectives were met.
- Students will have a mental plan for how to manage the classroom.

Structuring Your Class

Who are your students?

Before you can begin creating your class, you have to think about the class structure. Who are you going to teach? Women? Children? Men? Mothers and daughters? Mixed classes? This may matter because children have a shorter attention span than adults. Classes that include them may have to be shorter in duration. They will certainly require different types of learning activities. You may want to modify the type of music you use for this class as well.

I taught classes to people ages thirteen and over. I chose age thirteen as the cut off because my classes are fairly focused, and I didn't want students to be disturbed if another child got restless or had to go to the bathroom. Even though my cut-off was thirteen, the parents understood that if a child did not have the ability to concentrate for an entire hour, she would not be allowed to stay. I created my policies to address the learning needs for *most* of the students, and that worked for me.

Classes that include men may also be different from those that are women-only, because men's technique isn't exactly the same as women's. You will have to know both to teach to both genders. The number of people who are willing to take a mixed-gender class may influence your decision of who to include. Having a mixed-gender class may create possibilities and problems that don't exist in a single-gender class.

Men were permitted to attend my classes; however, I've never had more than two male students at a time. Attendees were aware that it was not a female-only class, however no one ever decided not to come for fear that a man might show up. The classroom had a serious atmosphere, so there wasn't time for checking each other out or worrying about whether the person next to you was a man or a woman; this simply didn't matter in my classes. In classes that are more social, it might be a consideration.

What about a class for seniors? The focus for seniors might be more recreational or exercise-driven. Most older people aren't striving for professional dance standards, so this class may have a more relaxed pace and be less physically strenuous than a class for younger students.

Where Are Your Classes Located?

Where will your class be held? If your classes are in your own studio, you have lots of options. If you are renting space or working for someone else, your options may be more limited, due to time and space. This factors into what you can plan because of time.

Looking Ahead…

You need to think beyond your first class or session. What will you do once your first class is over? Will you repeat the same class to different people? Will you teach the same level with different material? Will you add a class? Will you add another level?

It's easier to keep the students you have (assuming they are satisfied) than to try to get new ones. For that reason, if your classes are in sessions, you should figure out how to get the "graduating" students to stay. If you are doing classes for exercise, that's easy! You can just do what you were doing before and maybe change up the music and add a step or two. There is no expectation of learning technique or moving up a level, so as long as they are moving and having fun, your students will probably stick around. This logic also applies to classes that are geared towards self-esteem and fun.

If you are teaching beginners, the best thing to do is offer another beginner-level class that targets different aspects of beginning technique. Maybe you did a particular ten moves in the first class, and now you want to do the next ten. Or maybe you taught choreography to a Hakim song, and now you want to do one to a Light Rain song. The knowledge of technique continues to build, is still appropriate to that level, and therefore should be challenging. So these students should stay. It also allows for more students to join without having any previous knowledge of belly dance.

Regardless of the level of your students, consider beyond your first class. Think about your space, who your students are, retaining those students while growing your class size, and your capability of expanding, and use those factors to design a plan for the first class and beyond.

Pre-requisites, Testing, and Open Door Policy

Can anyone walk into your classes? Does your class require a pre-requisite? What about your more advanced classes? If there is a pre-requisite, how will you determine whether it has been met?

The value of an open door policy is that anyone can come. It completely takes the pressure off the student. Many students may be scared to death of doing new movements, showing off their bellies, and being seen as total klutzes. If they can just come, have fun, and have no standard to measure up to, your classes may be larger and more relaxed.

The downside is that you may have drastically different levels of students in the same class. This may make you work a lot harder. It can also lead to the more advanced students getting bored while you work on basic level material. If there are no codified standards to move up, your students may have no meaningful way of measuring progress. This can lead to a false sense of accomplishment, or it may make some students less motivated.

Pre-requisites are a way of controlling quality in the classroom. If everyone tests into a class or demonstrates a certain level of learning prior to starting a class, moving at a steady pace is much less of a problem.

My beginner level class was open to anyone. Advancing to the next level required knowledge of what I considered the foundation steps of belly dance. Each student had to test into that class and display that they understood my vocabulary, knew how to execute each movement, could perform beginner level choreography, could improvise, and could play a triplet on the zils. Students were scored on a Likert scale[1] of 0-2 for each tested movement. Each

---

[1] Likert scale is fully explained in chapter two.

criterion was weighted. Students had to score a 91% or better to pass. This gave me assurance that when each student passed into the next level, the class would not have to slow down for remedial instruction.

Maybe you don't want to run your classes this way. I am not suggesting that this works for everyone, as the overall goal for all of my classes was to teach students to dance Middle Eastern dance as a performing art to the best of their ability. The best way for me to achieve that was to test at each level. This gave me the confidence to pass them to the next level. This gave them a goal to work towards and put the responsibility on their shoulders to improve. You have to consider the overall goal of your program, as well as the goal of the class, when deciding whether to require pre-requisites and use testing.

Ongoing Classes or Sessions

Another thing to consider when structuring your classes is whether your classes are going to run in an ongoing manner or in sessions. If you decide on sessions, how many classes are in each session? How frequently do classes meet? How long is each class? The time allotted to teach a topic will determine the amount of depth you can give to the topic. Ongoing classes tend to be circular in design, doing A, then B, then A, then C, and moving in ways that loop around and around. Classes that move in sessions, on the other hand, tend to be more linear, following patterns that might look like this: A, B, AB, C, ABC, D, ABCD, etc..

My beginner class was ongoing. There were many practical reasons for doing it this way. I had a lot of military students who were not able to come regularly. Rather than turn them away or have them pay for a full session when they could only make one or two classes in the session, I used ongoing classes. This way they could drop in whenever they were in port and not really miss anything because the material was circular. There were six weeks of lessons, and then it started back at the beginning.

I also ran ongoing classes because I had students who could not afford to pay for the price of a session all at once. They could afford to pay for one class at a time. Even if it were only one class here and there, I'd rather have those people in class occasionally than have them miss out on the opportunity because of price. This may be more of an inconvenience than you want to deal with. If so, that's understandable. Everyone should consider her individual situation.

Sessions are a good idea financially. They make people commit to putting their money down. Whether that student decides to stay with the program or not, you still have their money! Students tend to stay with something they are financially invested in. If I pay $110 for an eight-week class, I am going to take eight weeks of lessons. If I pay $20 per class in a pay-as-you-go situation, it's a lot easier for me to skip weeks here and there to go bowling, watch a movie, or do any of the million things that come up in life.

When I first started dancing, I committed to eight weeks. Since I didn't know whether I would like belly dancing or not, it was hard for me to go week after week. It was summer. There were many other things I could have been doing. Had I not paid upfront, I very easily could have stopped going before I figured out whether or not belly dance was for me. Since I attended regularly, I got a chance to really get a feel for it and decide that I wanted to keep doing it. I think this made a big difference in my staying involved in belly dance.

Whether you decide to teach in sessions or ongoing classes, there has to be a definite beginning and end to the material. It's easier to know when you've gotten there in sessions because that usually coincides with the end of the session. It is probably a good idea to use some sort of testing-out process for students in an ongoing class, so that they have something to reach for and some way of knowing when they've achieved the goals of the class. If you require students to pass a test in order to move forward, psychologically prepare the students for the possibility that they may be repeating the session. There is nothing more disappointing than arriving at a destination and hearing that you have to go back while others go forward, if you were not prepared for that possibility beforehand.

Your Goal and Objectives

Before you can figure out your objectives or lesson plans, you have to know what your goal is. Your goal is what you hope to accomplish. This should be narrow enough to be accomplished in the time allowed, yet broad enough to give you several objectives. Usually this is one statement. Here are some examples of goals:

- This class will give students a working knowledge of using three finger cymbal patterns while moving.
- Students will have a working knowledge of fundamental belly dance movements.
- Students will be able to choreograph a dance to this piece of music.

I can check to see if this is a good goal by asking myself:

- Is this clearly stated in one idea?
- Is my idea concrete?
- Is it measurable?
- Do I have the ability to do this?
- Do I have the tools to do this?
- Do my students have the skills they need to do this?

If you can answer yes to all these questions, you probably have a good goal.

Once you have determined the goal of your class, you can set objectives. Objectives describe how you hope to accomplish the goal. So a goal is where you want to go, and the objectives are how you are going to get there. Without objectives, it's like saying, "I want to go to Japan" and then taking off in a car, boat, plane, or on foot and hoping that you arrive!

If I used the first example of, "This class will give students a working knowledge of three finger cymbal patterns," my objectives could be:

- Students will be able to play a triplet while dancing.
- Students will be able to play the Beledi pattern while dancing.
- Students will be able to play a pattern of 3s and 7s while dancing.

I can check to see if my objectives are good ones by asking myself, "If my student did these things successfully, is it reasonable for them to accomplish this goal?" If the answer is no, your objectives either need to be restated or more objectives should be added. So, if there were only two objectives (playing a triplet while dancing and playing Beledi while dancing) and my goal was to have them play three finger cymbal patterns, it should be pretty obvious that another pattern needs to be added in order to meet the goal of having three patterns. If the objectives were the same, and the goal was to play improvisationally, I may fail to meet my goal because the objectives do not necessarily have anything to do with playing improvisationally.

I cannot overstate how useful goals and objectives are to your teaching. If you don't know where you are going, you can't know when you have arrived. If you don't have a written plan, it may not be easy to see where you went wrong. If you have written goals and objectives, it's a lot easier to repeat success by using the same techniques that you did before.

Having written goals and objectives gives you a way to maximize success the first time you try something new. Have you ever learned something new or had a bright idea and then tried it and it totally bombed? If you write it out, you can more easily see where things might fall apart and correct it beforehand. Teaching becomes less risky with a plan.

When things don't go as planned, goals and objectives give you a place to start looking for what went wrong so that you can fix it. Perhaps you didn't actually carry out your plan. Perhaps your material failed to achieve the objective. Perhaps X took a lot longer to execute than anticipated, so you didn't have time to get to Y. Perhaps you did everything just as you should have, but the students didn't reach the goal because there were other skills that they needed first. Perhaps the material wasn't delivered in a way that was effective. Maybe you were just hungry and not focused, so things came out kind of jumbled. There are a million things that can go wrong, especially when teaching a new class. If you compare what happened to what you had planned, this can make it a lot easier to change course and get it right the second time.

So let's take another look at the above goals and objectives and figure out how the plan could be executed.

Goal: This class will give students a working knowledge of three finger cymbal patterns

Objectives:
• Students will be able to play a triplet while dancing.
• Students will be able to play the Beledi pattern while dancing.
• Students will be able to play a pattern of 3s and 7s while dancing.

My plan might begin with teaching the first pattern at half the speed. I could let the student walk with that (because to me, "working knowledge" means that they can not only play it, but also move with it). Then I would have the student do it at full tempo. Then the student could walk with that. Then I would have the student do some simple dance movements with that. Then I might add the second finger cymbal pattern, and then repeat the sequence. Then I might add the third and repeat that sequence. By breaking up the goal into bite-sized pieces, I have made it easier to achieve. If I spread those steps out over a period of weeks, by the end of the session, my students should have accomplished the goals and objectives for this class. See how easy that was?

More Examples of Goals and Objectives

Actually it's not "easy" to create useful goals and objectives. Some seasoned teachers have trouble with it, so let's walk through a few examples to give you some practice.

Example One

Let's say that you always find yourself late and this is negatively impacting your job. You tend to stay up too late. You are a heavy sleeper who takes a while to get up. You need coffee in the morning or else you are a bear. You also have to drop off your child at the daycare on the way to work, which is on the other side of town.

That's a lot to deal with, but our first step is to figure out what the problem is. Despite all that information, the problem isn't how late you go to sleep. It isn't that you are not a morning person. It isn't that you need coffee or that your sitter is on the other side of town. The problem is that you are habitually late to work. We want the goal to solve the problem. So our goal statement is: I will be on time to work. (Goal= *what* you want to accomplish).

Okay, how are you going to do that? Well, we have a lot of information, and therefore a lot of ways to tackle the problem. Our objective is *how* you are going to accomplish the goal.

Here are some examples:

• I will start winding down by 9:00 p.m.
• I will be physically in bed by 10:00 p.m.
• I will turn out the lights and try to sleep by 10:30 p.m.
• I will set the alarm three minutes earlier than I have been.
• I will set the coffee maker timer so that it is ready when I wake up.
• I will leave the house at least fifteen minutes earlier than normal.

If I fail to do just one thing on my list of objectives, it may or may not influence my success. However, if I don't do one or two things, and then don't have the success I am looking for, that gives me a place to start when revising my objectives.

On the other hand, if I do all of the things on my list of objectives and get to work on time, that tells me that my plan works. This suggests that if I do it again the next time, it will work then, too.

Example Two

Now let's look at a dance example.

You are designing a two-hour sword workshop for people with limited sword experience. Since the class is only two hours, you have to be particular about what you can share. You want the students to feel confident with the sword, be able to do a few sword moves, and take something concrete home with them to practice.

To figure out a goal, first you have to decide what the problem is. In this case, the problem is that you have new students with little sword experience.

Next, you have to decide what you hope to accomplish. The goal is (you can state this as the student's goal or as your goal): "Students will gain familiarity with the sword, as demonstrated by their ability to do a few standard movements." The "as demonstrated by" statement is added, because if you only said, "Students will gain familiarity with the sword," there is really no objective way to measure if that goal was met. You might think it definitely was, while I might think it definitely wasn't, and the student may have an opinion that is somewhere in between. Making it concrete removes the guesswork.

So, how do I hope to accomplish that? In other words, what are my objectives?

- Students will spin the sword in their hands.
- Students will balance the sword on various parts of their bodies.
- Students will demonstrate handling the sword in various ways.
- Students will put the moves together in a two-minute choreography.

If the members of my class practice spinning the sword in their hands, would that help them "gain a familiarity with the sword"? Would it help them "do a few standard movements"? What about having students practice balancing the sword on various parts of their bodies? What about having them practice different ways of handling the sword? What about using those movements in a two-minute choreography? Yes, all of those things would help them to gain familiarity with the sword and do a few standard movements.

This plan works on paper, so it's ready to try it out in the real world. Things don't always go as planned. There may need to be some tweaking yet, but at least we have a reasonable starting place.

Example Three

Now let's use a dance example that's not so simple.

There is a holiday showcase coming up with a group choreography in which everyone participates. There are six solo slots. There is a lottery system in which those who want to solo can put their name in a hat for a random chance at getting one of four solo slots. The other two slots are meritorious.

Hadia, Nadia, and Badia all started dancing at the same time and have been dancing at this studio longer than anyone else. They all want to get a solo slot and feel that their best chance is to be chosen for the meritorious ones, because otherwise, they are competing with about twenty-five other dancers. Hadia is clearly the most technically skilled dancer of the three, but she tends to be late for class, misses class, and doesn't pay on time. She sometimes misses performances without advance notice. Nadia is the least technically skilled, but is the most passionate. She works hard, pays for private tutoring, practices intensely, and has lovely costuming. She volunteers for every performance opportunity, shows up on time, and performs to the best of her ability each time. Badia is the middle of the road dancer. She is naturally gifted, so she doesn't study particularly hard. Her technical skill is fine, but not superb. Her artistry is where she excels. She can make the audience cry with her intensity. Badia doesn't make every performance, because her work and family life do not permit it. However, if she commits, she shows up and does a good job.

What is the problem here? Is it that there are two open dance slots and three good dancers? No. That's how the problem manifests, but the problem is that there is no way of objectively deciding who should get those meritorious slots. There is no definition of what meritorious means. This is a policy issue, not a dance issue, but it is one that could come up in a classroom situation.

My goal (what I want to accomplish) is: Solo performers for the holiday show will be chosen based on objective standards for two solo slots.

How do I do this? In other words, what are my objectives?

- Create a point system for acknowledging when dancers meet certain objectives, like being on time, paying on time, performing, volunteering, etc.
- Measure these objectives starting three months prior to the holiday show.
- Post the point system so that dancers can see where they stand and possibly change their standing.
- Award the dance slots one month before the show, based on the number of points each dancer earns.

Using goals and objectives makes it a lot easier to see and think clearly. It helps you get where you are going without getting side tracked. They can be applied to lesson planning, creating a class, deciding whether or not you want to teach at all, and many other aspects of your life.

Writing Your Course Description

The course description tells your students what to expect from class. It is used to advertise the course and attract people to your class. Colleges, recreation centers, gyms, and other organizations use them. It's a good idea that you have one in writing, too, so that you can succinctly tell people what they can expect to learn.

Here are some examples of real course descriptions for dance classes:

"Zaina's" classes are small group ensuring individual attention for all students. These classes are American cabaret and Arabic styles-with a pinch of Latin and East Indian flavor. In addition these classes prepare the body for dance, facilitating understanding choreography, providing costuming tips, and performance technique."

"This class is for the many people who call us and say, "I have two left feet." It's ideal for the person who has never had dance instruction and would like to learn the proper way to dance. Remember, there are only two ways: right and wrong. The basic steps, timing, and character will be taught in each class."

"Belly dancing is an exciting Middle Eastern dance relying on movement handed down from generation to generation from ancient times to the present. You will learn the beautiful and spectacular veil dance, as well as slow and fast body isolations and rhythms. You will learn slow figure eights of the entire body, hips, and torso, as well as soft and flowing hand and arm moves. In this class you will learn to put together your own routine and develop your own style. Improve muscle tone and flexibility, gain body awareness and self-confidence, and get quite a workout! All body types and ages welcome!"

"Have a blast with your friends in this energetic hip hop class, systematically designed to warm you up and make you sweat! Learn exciting choreography by breaking down steps, practicing them at half time and adding on gradually, until you are moving like your favorite music video star! Dancers will absolutely enjoy this class that will challenge their skills."

I share these examples so that you can see the wide variety of styles people use in writing course descriptions. Many belly dancers use course descriptions that are vague, sound unprofessional, and use poor grammar. That is one of the things that keep us the stepsister of the dance world. A good class description lets your personality show. This will help you attract students who fit in your class, but still let you maintain your professionalism. An effective course description should hint at the seriousness of the class and tell students what they can hope to achieve there.

In the first example, there is little attention to detail. The words don't flow, and it looks like the writer was in a hurry. The reader may come away with the thought that this class offers individual attention and has fusion, but if she feels professionalism is more important than those benefits, she will probably look elsewhere for an instructor. This is an easily avoided way to lose students. Don't let this happen to you.

The second class description sounds like it was written by someone who is hard core. He/she says there is a right way and a wrong way! This class sounds like you will get serious technique. It sounds like the instructor cares about teaching properly, but there is no hint of humor or fun in this class.

The third class description falls again into the unprofessional belly dancer stereotype. The sentences are too long and exaggerated. An experienced dancer would think to herself, "My, this is a lot to expect from a seven week class," so she's not likely to attend. Are the hips and torso not included in the "whole body"? This doesn't flow. It sounds like the writer was trying to put too much into the class and the description. At best, it sounds like an unskilled writer. At worst it sounds like an unskilled instructor!

The final example has life. The class sounds easy and fun. It makes you want to sign up right now. The reader gets the idea that this class is a fun workout that will teach something. This is a good class description. Not too long. Not too exaggerated. And it reflects the personality of the teacher.

Ultimately, the description should be a reflection of what you plan to teach and who you are. Some people want exercise. Some people want to develop their technique. Some want to work their creative side. If you word your course description in a way that accurately describes your class, you will have a much better chance of attracting the student who will benefit most from what you have to offer. If you do this in an unprofessional way, you are more likely to lose the prospect than gain her.

This isn't intended to be a creative writing class, but do pay attention to what you put out there. Describe what the student will learn. Give a feel for the atmosphere. Tell them who this class is targeted to. Tell them about the benefits of being in class. Avoid hyperbole. Keep it short and sweet and grammatically correct. And proof read it!

Creating Lesson Plans

Now that you know who's coming to your class, where it will be held, whether it is going to be in sessions or ongoing, what skill level it is targeted to, and what the goals and objectives are, you can write your lesson plan. Your lesson plan outlines what you are going to teach and how you are going to teach it.

I will illustrate this by doing a lesson plan with you. Here is what I am going to consider before setting about planning how to teach:

Who am I teaching? *Beginner level students, male and female, over thirteen*

What am I teaching? *Beginner level fundamentals*

Any pre-requisites required? *No*

What is the class structure? *Ongoing, weekly, drop-ins allowed*

Goal: *Students will have a working knowledge of the foundations of belly dance* (Notice that this is one idea. A vague one, but only one. My objectives will make it concrete and measurable.)

Objectives: *Students will be able to put names with movement, execute beginner movements in isolation, perform a one minute choreography, be able to improvise for one minute, and play a triplet pattern while moving*

What tools will I need to do this? *Handout with the names of the movements, handout of the goals and objectives, written choreography notes, dry erase board with choreography steps written on it for in-class use, music, sound equipment, finger cymbals, flash cards, assessment*

What is my time frame for accomplishing this goal? *Unlimited, classes are ongoing*

From here, you are going to take the objectives and put them into action steps. Based on this, here is what students have to accomplish and how I plan to help them do it.

Identify moves by name: I will give students a list of movements I consider "basic" and refer to these movements by name in class as they are drilled. I may also use the dry erase board to write them down, so that students can learn to associate the movements with the names. I may also use flash cards to quiz or cue them.

Perform the movements in isolation: I will break down and drill these movements in class in isolation.

Use the movements in a short choreography: I have to create this choreography, teach it to the class, and write choreography notes so that students can practice it at home.

Use the movements in improvisation: Students can use the choreography as a framework for how to string movements together. I will also combine smooth moves during the smooth move class, percussive moves during the percussive class, and traveling steps during that class. This will help them to develop transition skills needed to improvise. All classes end with a "free dance" in which the students can follow me or do their own thing.

Play finger cymbals while moving: I will show students how to play a triple and practice it with them while standing still and moving. I will also play at half time and full time.

Now I just have to put these thoughts into a plan that flows at a pace that is neither too fast nor too slow. Before I put my thoughts into a plan, I have to consider what other factors may come into play, such as students who start at different times. I have to keep things interesting so that the students will stay with it. I have to repeat things often enough that the learning is reinforced, but not so often that class is boring. I have to give my students a way of evaluating their progress. With that in mind, here is my plan.

Lesson A: Total Review

What	Description
Warm-up	Segues into movement rehearsal
Frames	
Smooth moves	wrist circles, snake arms, Hindu arms, butterfly hands, chest circles, undulations, amis, vertical and horizontal figure eights
Percussive moves	head slides, shoulder shimmies, chest lifts/drops, m & m, shimmies, ¾ shimmies, hip drop/lift, yes-I-do
Traveling steps	step-together-step, big stroke little stroke, grapevine, basic Egyptian, basic Arabic, pony, Tunisian, double Tunisian, Ghawazee, three point turn, butterfly turn, paddle turn, Arabic 6, box step, karsilama step
Free dance	5 minutes or so
Cool down	5 minutes or so

Lesson B: Percussion

What	Description
Warm-up	Segues into lesson, entire segment is 45 minutes
Review moves	head slides, shoulder shimmies, chest lifts/drops, m & m, shimmies, 3/4 shimmies, hip drop/lift, yes-I-do
Combos	
Improvise	
Review choreography	2 run throughs, 5 minutes
Free dance	Use percussive music to encourage percussive practice
Cool down	About 5 minutes

Lesson C: Drum Solo Choreography

What	Description
Warm-up	Segues into choreography lesson
Choreography	
Free dance	5 minutes
Cool down	5 minutes

Lesson D: Traveling steps

What	Description
Warm-up	Segues into traveling lesson, 35 minutes total
Review steps	step-together-step, big stroke little stroke, grapevine, basic Egyptian, basic Arabic, pony, Tunisian, double Tunisian, Ghawazee, three point turn, butterfly turn, paddle turn, Arabic 6, box step, karsilama step
Create combinations	10 minutes
Free dance	5 minutes
Cool down	5 minutes

Lesson E: Finger cymbals

What	Description
Warm-up	Segues into finger cymbal lesson, 45 minutes total
Zil lesson	Play triplet pattern slowly and in isolation, then at half time, then full speed. Add walking, then while doing a traveling step or two
Review drum solo choreography	5 minutes
Free dance	5 minutes
Cool down	5 minutes

Lesson F: Smooth Moves

What	Description
Warm-up	Segues into lesson, 35 minutes total
Review steps	wrist circles, snake arms, Hindu arms, butterfly hands, chest circles, undulations, amis, vertical and horizontal figure eights
Create combinations	10 minutes
Free dance	5 minutes
Cool down	5 minutes

Once the cycle finishes, it simply repeats.

Although the curriculum is ambitious, there is plenty of time for review. New students can start at any time and catch up easily, because each class starts with a break down of movement in isolation. Students who have been there a while will have the opportunity to master their isolations by using them in combinations. All will have a chance to "play" during the free dance. Even though some movements are not concentrated on for weeks, they are seen in the choreography and weekly in the free dance. There is also an optional video that students may purchase to review all the moves at home on their own.

When students are ready to test out of the class, they make an appointment with me outside of class time. I read down the list of movements then check off whether they performed it correctly. Then I put on a random piece of music that they have heard before in class and ask them to dance for one minute. They also have to perform the drum solo alone. Next they dance to something of their choice while playing finger cymbals for one minute.

The choreography, improvisation, and finger cymbal playing are each 10% of the scoring. The movements are 70%. They must achieve a 91% or higher to pass (which means they must pass the choreography, improvisation, and finger cymbal elements). Although this may seem like a high bar, I have found that when students are allowed to pass with a lower score, they do not work on their own to perfect the movements that were not up to par. Since I cannot slow down the class for remedial work, this could mean that they continue to reinforce bad habits and accept technique that's not outstanding.

The students are given the scored assessment sheet at the end of the test, so they know exactly what they have to work on. If they pass, they can move to the next level. If they don't pass, they have to take the entire test again when they are ready.

To reduce the fear, I tell everyone that the first test is for practice. It's just a review to familiarize them with the test process. This sets the norm that no one passes the first time. If they don't pass, it is no big deal. If they do, they are delighted.

Review Your Plan

Once you create your plan, make sure to review it to see if all your objectives support goal attainment. If not, take something out, add something, or rewrite it.

Check to see if you have given yourself an action plan for how to bring your objectives to life. If you say you are going to teach students how to play a triple, is that actually in the lesson plan?

Do you have enough time to accomplish everything? I have seen lesson plans like the one listed above that are designed for newcomers to complete in eight weeks. This is not a realistic time line. If the goal were to have an introduction to belly dance, that could work as an overview, but it wouldn't work if students were expected to "get" it after eight weeks.

Have you built in enough review and repetition to solidify the instruction? I've seen far more ambitious lesson plans than those which don't challenge the student enough. Repetition is required to make correct movement habitual. Some teachers fear that this is boring. Anything can be presented in a way that is fun, if you employ a little creativity. What makes it boring is you! If you are not boring, your material won't be either.

Test Your Plan

Once you are satisfied that the plan looks solid, test it. Run with it and review your results. Take notes. If you planned to do X on the first week, but only got through half of that material, that's good feedback. It could mean that your pacing is too slow, the material is too hard, your teaching technique needs some changes, your classroom management skills are being challenged, or any number of things.

If you went through the entire lesson plan without a hitch and your goals were not accomplished, look to see what you could do to strengthen the plan. If you went through the entire lesson plan and your goals were accomplished, add enhancements, and run it again so that the next time it's even better.

Enhance Your Plan

Some people have the mentality of, "If it ain't broke, don't fix it". That's fine. Quality improvement is not part of everyone's plan and some people don't want to work that hard. I get that. But I don't think you would be interested in learning to teach the BDT way if that were your mentality.

When I think of that person, I think of the teacher who has been teaching the same choreographies for the last ten years. There's nothing wrong with that. A thing of beauty is a joy forever (Keats), but it can look like a dated thing of beauty. And if it's been seen over and over by the same people, it can be a bit stale.

I prefer the mentality of constant improvement. You have the potential to grow every time you teach a class. From every class you teach, you get feedback that can make your instruction more dynamic, clearer, and inspiring. If you incorporate that feedback into your written plan, you won't forget those gems of insight. Instead of teaching habitually, you will teach in a more enlightened way. This keeps it fresh, alive, and new for everyone.

Creating Your Assessment Tools

I've talked around assessment tools, but I haven't actually explained them or told you how to create them yet. So what's an assessment tool? How do you know if it's objective? And how do you know if it is measuring what you want it to measure? There are entire courses on that alone, but here is a basic rundown.

Remember back in primary school when you took tests that were True or False, multiple choice, or matching? Those are assessment tools. Assessment tools are instruments that are designed to provide information. Perhaps the goal is to see how fast you can type. Maybe the purpose is to see what level of understanding you have in algebra. Maybe it's designed to see how many calories you burn while dancing. Assessment tools can gather all sorts of data. In this particular instance, we want to measure a student's dance knowledge.

Designing tools that measure what they say they are measuring is a specialty that some people study for a long time. It's far beyond the scope of this program to get into that, but there are some basic things you can look for that will hint as to whether your assessment instrument is valid.

True/False

First, does the information have one right answer? If it does, then a True or False test could be the way to measure it. The trick to this is designing unambiguous test questions that focus on the body of knowledge that you are measuring.

For example: An objective way to pose this statement on a True/False test would be: "The karsilama rhythm uses a 9/8 time signature." That answer is true. There is no other answer, so that's a good test question.

Here's an example of a poor test question: "Ghawazee dancers wear short dresses." That answer is sometimes true. It depends on what time period you are talking about, so that is not an effective question. It doesn't have one correct answer.

Here's another example of a poor test question: "Nagwa Fouad is the best Egyptian dancer of all time." That's clearly subjective. Each person answering that question could have different responses, so this is not a valid test question.

When using True/False tests, the statements *must be* objective and have *one* right answer. This type of test is good for testing knowledge of details. Since most dance classes do not focus on objective things like culture and history, this assessment tool would probably not be widely used.

Multiple Choice

Multiple choice tests are also used for measuring knowledge of details. A multiple choice question looks like this:

"Tonya and Atlantis sponsor this belly dance competition: _____"
a) Jewel of the Nile
b) The East Coast Belly Dance Classic
c) Belly Dancer of the Universe
d) Cleopatra

It is possible to use an instrument like this for testing dance knowledge, but again, since we are usually testing for conceptual knowledge, not factual knowledge, this probably would not be widely used.

Matching

If you are teaching a class on rhythms, you may want to use matching to see if the student has an intellectual understanding of the material. Matching uses a word or phrase on one side of the page and definitions or things that are association with those words or phrases on the other. The student pairs them up in ways that make sense. Here is an example:

Match the rhythm with the country where it is typically found

1. Egyptian   a. Karachi
2. Pakistani   b. Chifti-telli
3. Turkish   c. Bolero
                   d. Masmoodi

Although matching works to show factual knowledge, I think it is more valuable to have the student hear the music and match it somehow that way, rather than put words and phrases together. Using the ear, which is how music is used, is a more meaningful way to express music. That should be considered when deciding upon which assessment tools you will use. Which tool gives you the most information and/or the most meaningful information?

Although it may seem that True/False, multiple choice, and matching are not tools that would be used in a belly dance class, this is not completely true. If you are teaching in a venue that requires testing, such as a university or grade school, this is often the type of test that is encouraged.

Essay

True/False, multiple choice, and matching are good for testing objective information, but what if you are interested in subjective information? A good way to see the complexity of a student's understanding is to use an essay test. Questions can be targeted to specific information or be open-ended. For example, you could instruct the student to, "Compare and contrast Turkish and Egyptian styles of dance." This statement looks for specific information and will illuminate the student's understanding of both styles of dance in a way that True/False, multiple choice, and matching cannot.

Here's another example of an open-ended essay: "Explain the basic elements of choreography and how each is used."

While essays are great for gaining a detailed understanding of the student's knowledge, they are more time intensive to grade. In order to get consistency in grading, you have to know what the expected answers are in advance and give each answer a weighted score. You have to pre-determine how you will score extraneous and/or erroneous information. As you can see, unless you are skilled at creating and assessing essays, the scoring can be wildly unreliable.

Another consideration when testing subjective information is how to measure it. If the goals of your class are to increase self-esteem and enhance self-awareness, how will you measure that? Will this be judged by your observation? By the student's self-report? If you are basing this on your observation, what criteria are you looking for? Smiling more? Being more assertive? Better posture? A willingness to dance in front of other people? It's very tricky judging subjective things like those, because there is lots of variety in how people express internal states. I could be incredibly happy without showing any outward signs. I could also be irritated without your knowledge.

What if you rely on self-report? Do people always tell the truth? Are your questions worded in such a way that they reveal what you are looking for? Subjective goals are not as easy to measure as objective ones. This doesn't mean that they should not be included in the goals of your class. It just means that if subjective gains are the basis of your business, you have to get creative in how you design your assessment tool, because it will be of little value if the results aren't valid.

Likert Scale

What I use for evaluating the objectives for the beginner's class I previously described is a Likert scale. A Likert scale is a measuring instrument that is graduated. It has numbers to indicate varying degrees of something. The Likert scale is supposed to be a four to ten point rating scale, but for my beginner class I used a scale of 0-2. If the student is asked to perform a figure eight (for example), and she does a hip circle, she would score a 0. If she does something that looks like a figure eight, but isn't quite technically correct, she'd get a 1. If she understands what the word figure eight means and executes it well, she'd get a 2. So a 0 means that the student doesn't know what the word means and cannot execute the movement. A 1 means that the student probably knows what the word means, but cannot properly execute the movement. A 2 means that the student understands the word and how to execute the movement, which was the goal. In order to be useful, the scores should be fully defined so that anyone who views them at any point in time will be able to understand the meaning of the score.

This is far less subjective than looking at a student and saying, "Yes, she understands 91% of what I was trying to teach." The only way to truly know that is to write it down and score each skill.

Here is an example of a Likert scale:

0- did not execute: Student either did no movement or did a movement that was not the named movement
1- partially executed: Student's movement was technically incorrect
2- executed: Student executed the movement correctly

Hip circle	1	Hip lift	2
Snake arms	2	Undulation	1
Hip drop	0	Ami	2

Checklist

Another assessment tool is a checklist. If we are studying tribal style, for example, and the objectives are to know when to transition, know how to cue, and know five basic tribal steps, I could watch the dancer dance and check off the box if she properly executes those things.

Here's an example of a checklist:

____ transitions on the "1"
__X_ cues are visible
____ cues are within the defined tribal vocabulary
____ accurately performs Arabic
__X_ accurately performs an undulation

Obviously, lesson plans and assessment tools vary widely. Yours do not have to look anything like mine. As long as you have a lesson plan that suits the skill level of the students, can be accomplished in the given amount of time, and teaches what it sets out to teach, your lesson plan is probably a good one. If your assessment tool is objective, provides you and the student with useful feedback, measures what it's supposed to measure, and scores each student by the same criteria, it's probably a good one.

You do not have to use assessment tools to teach the Belly Dance Trainer way, but it helps tremendously. If you choose to have students participate in an assessment, know that there are some students who will not want to be in your class. Maybe they are only interested in having fun. Maybe they just want a workout. Maybe they do not want to be judged. Assessments are not a good choice for every class.

Also be aware that even when they are a good idea, there may be students who think more highly of their skills than you do and will resent having their skills honestly assessed. If you choose to assess skill level and require that a certain skill level be obtained before students can pass to the next level, you have to be strong enough to stick to your guidelines. Students will resent it if everyone is not held to the same rules. If the goal is learning and excellence, students will produce for you and themselves if they know that their hard work will be recognized.

Even if you decide not to subject *students* to assessment, you may wish to still use them to critique yourself, your program, or your lesson plan. For example, let's say that you don't subject students in your beginning class to an assessment because the goal of the class is to gain self-esteem and relieve stress. However, you observe and document how many people accomplished X, Y, and Z, because this gives you information on whether or not your teaching methods are working. You also gather data on how many people drop out and at what point they drop out. If you learn that 25% drop out at the halfway point, perhaps something that you are teaching in the class just before that point is not pleasant. Or maybe the sessions are too long.

Data gathering may be tedious and boring, but it provides important information about your class and your teaching. It indicates when your plan needs revision. It can tell you that your plan is working. Once you hit on a plan that gets the results you want, your students will be happy because they are excelling. Your classes will remain full. You will gain more students because the ones you have will tell others. And you have less work to do because the plan is already created. All you have to do is execute it.

Assessment data even provides you with a road map for "what next?" Instead of simply adding another choreography class because your demand is high and class offerings are low, you can add a class with the intention of providing your students with the next step in their growth.

Perhaps the best reason to consider using assessments is that they keep you and your students from stagnating. Change is vital to the health of your business. Incremental changes towards excellence can produce groundbreaking results so gradually and easily that it won't feel like work.

Creating Policies

Good teachers create class policies to prevent problems from occurring. When students and parents are aware of what the policies are in advance, there is less chance for issues to arise because an understanding is created *at the beginning* of the relationship. While policies can be created informally through behavior, it is best to have written polices that are shared with the students on the first day of class.

When creating policies, you should consider your personality, the students, and the goals of the class. If you are a relaxed and easy-going person, you may have a hard time enforcing rules that you think you *should* have, but don't really believe in. This will undermine you in the long run, because you will eventually lose respect if you don't enforce your own rules. You will also have a hard time feeling good about something your heart doesn't believe in. So make sure that your policies are a reflection of you.

If you teach children, the policies for that class will certainly be different from a class full of professional adults. Students who are there for recreation may also be held to a different standard than those who are there to become performers. Make sure that your policy is appropriate for the commitment level of your class. There is no hard and fast rule that policies must be a certain way, so take your time in developing what works best for you.

You may wish to incorporate ethics into your policies for performance students. There are many students who are not aware of the standard ethical practices of professional dancers. They may not know, for example, that it's considered professional to respect colleagues or charge a fair wage. Your responsibility as an instructor goes far beyond dance. It includes grooming students to be courteous and professional, so that when they are seen in public representing Middle Eastern dance, it is always portrayed in a positive light. This may seem like it goes without saying. But the abundance of students who undercut, "steal" jobs, and talk badly about others who are perceived as competition points to the lack of instruction in this area.

Be sure to remember that just because something isn't a problem today, doesn't mean it won't happen at some time in the future. Think proactively. It's much easier to create a policy today than to have to deal with a problem later for which there was no written policy.

Your basic policies for a beginner class will likely include issues like:

- attendance
- tardiness
- payment

- dress code
- class observation
- drop-ins
- classroom behavior
- cancellation
- performances
- intellectual property
- advancement
- termination

There may be additional topics that fit your situation that aren't listed here. You may have different policies for performance level classes than non-performance classes. Your policies for a troupe may be different. If you employ other teachers, you would have policies governing that relationship. You want to create a separate policy for each situation. Obtain a signed copy for yourself that you keep on file, and give a copy to the student. If the student is a minor, be sure to have the parent sign.

Example of Policies

Attendance

It is the student's responsibility to know when and where the class takes place. Regular attendance is required to progress. Students will not get a refund for missed classes. Make-up classes are not offered at this time.

Tardiness

Classes will start on time. Students are expected to be timely. Should a student arrive late, she is to enter unobtrusively, warm herself up at the back of the class, and join the class at the back of the room once she is warmed up.

Payment

Payment is due in full prior to the end of the first class of the session. Payment may be made by cash, check, money order, or credit card. The fee for returned checks is $35. Should a check be returned for non-payment of funds, that student must pay by cash from that date forward. In order to keep costs low, we do not have provisions for billing students in arrears. Payments must be current in order to stay in class. No refunds are given if the session has already started.

Dress Code

Student shall wear clothing that is comfortable to move in, but does not inhibit the instructor from seeing the movement. Students shall be dressed in a modest fashion at all times. Dance shoes are recommended.

Class Observers

We have a "no observers" policy. Should someone wish to "try the class out" we offer a free introductory class once every other month that those people are invited to attend.

Drop-ins

Drop-ins may attend the Foundations class at a fee of $X. Drop-ins are not permitted to attend any other class.

Classroom Behavior

The goal of this school is to teach students to dance; therefore, cross talk while class is in session should be kept to a minimum. Direct all questions involving technique to the instructor. If students have questions they want to ask in private, the instructor is available for ten minutes before and after class and by email.

Disruptive behavior will not be tolerated.

Disrespectful behavior will not be tolerated. If students develop personality conflicts or have other personal issues with each other or the instructor, those problems will not be brought into the classroom.

This school has a no-discrimination policy. We do not discriminate against any student, staff member, or guest on the basis of color, religion, race, national origin, sexual orientation, weight, or age. Discriminatory practices shall not be tolerated.

No gum or food shall be consumed in the classroom. Bottled water is permitted.

Students who appear intoxicated or impaired shall not be permitted to attend class that day.

Cancellation

There will be times when it is necessary to cancel class. If an entire session is canceled, the staff will attempt to notify students by phone or email at least one week in advance. Should a single class during a session need to be canceled due to inclement weather, no make-up class will be scheduled. No refund will be due. An attempt will be made to notify students in advance. If you do not get a call, call the studio. If a live person is not available, there will be a voice mail message about the class cancellation.

Should a single class during a session need to be canceled due to an instructor emergency, a substitute teacher will be sought. If none is found, class will be canceled. A make-up class will be scheduled at a time that is convenient for the teacher. No refund will be due. An attempt will be made to notify students in advance.

Performances

This studio offers an annual recital in which all students may participate. Other performance opportunities may also arise. All performances are optional. Those who agree to participate must be currently enrolled in class, have their tuition paid up to date, must attend all rehearsals unless excused by the director, and have the required costuming.

Intellectual Property

Students understand that all choreographies taught at this studio are the intellectual property of the studio and may not be used outside of class without the copyright holder's written permission.

Advancement

Students are advanced to the next level once they have accomplished the objectives of each level. Students must "test out" to move to the next level. Once they've tested out, they can join the new class at the beginning of the next session.

Termination

Students may terminate their relationship with this studio at any time for any reason by not showing up and stopping payment of tuition. Students may be suspended or expelled from class for disruptive behavior or non-payment of tuition. Should a student be suspended or expelled for non-payment of tuition, the student will remain responsible for that debt. If a student is terminated for cause, reinstatement shall be considered on a case-by-case basis.

Managing Your Classroom

If you sign on to any belly dance forum, bulletin board, or group that deals with teaching, you will see questions about how to manage a classroom. There is nothing wrong with seeking help with a problem. Being prepared with strategies for dealing with problems prior to teaching will help you to avoid them in the first place. That's what this section is about:

How to manage your classroom to avoid and deal with problems

Let's begin with the teaching area itself. If you are teaching in someone else's space, like a fitness studio, rented space, or yoga studio, you will want to know what equipment is available to you, how to access it and work it, and who to contact if there should be a problem. You also need to be aware of the rules for using that space. Usually you will get an introduction to the space that will resolve all these issues for you, but if you don't, ask for the information. You don't want to meet for your first class and discover that you can't unlock the cabinet where the sound system is stored. You don't want to find yourself in a boiling room with no way to control the temperature.

While I am speaking about temperature, the atmosphere of the space should also be considered. Make sure that the temperature is comfortable for a moving body to work in. Be certain that the floor is clean and free of any obstacles. Is there enough light? Are there mirrors? It is the teacher's job to provide a physical atmosphere that gives the students the best chance to concentrate and learn.

The next consideration is emotional atmosphere. The energy should have, at minimum, a vibration of respect. If students feel uncomfortable, combative, edgy, or negative in any way, it won't be easy to control the classroom. You create the atmosphere of the room with your policies and your demeanor. If you are respectful, your students will be too. If you are happy and joyous, your students will be too. If you allow negative talk about other instructors or dancers, you will perpetuate that in class. Preventing negativity is a lot easier than squashing it once it's in full bloom, so be careful of the vibe that you create and allow to flourish.

Sometimes disruption cannot be avoided and we have to deal with it head on. When faced with a problem, here is how I typically approach it. First, I will determine if this is indeed a problem. Then I will discuss possible solutions with the person or people who can resolve it. Remember that every problem and solution will be unique to the situation because of the individuals involved, their relationships, and the mores of the classroom, so these are not intended to be one-size-fits-all solutions.

Situation One: *A student comes early to class every week and waits in the lobby for class to begin. While talking with other students, she complains about her marriage, her work, her kids, and her life. She brings this into the classroom. Others are complaining about it.*

This is a problem because this student is not here to dance. Or if she is, she doesn't recognize how her talking is keeping her and everyone else from learning how to dance. Her focus is on herself. She's not respecting that there is a time to share personal issues, and this is not it.

To break her of this chatter, make sure that class has a definite beginning. You can signal this by closing the door, ringing a bell, entering the classroom for the first time, or doing some other habitual thing that says, "We are starting class now." Having a starting ritual sends a signal that it's time for students to turn their attention to class. Continue the ritual with your warm-up. The warm up should focus on mentally and physically preparing the class for dance. There are many ways to do this and how you do it is up to you. Here is what I do.

I start the class by breathing. I do this because many students do not know how to breathe and this gets them thinking about it. It conditions them to begin to breathe with movement. It also quiets them and centers their energy on the here and now. When they are focused on breathing, they are no longer thinking about traffic, the weather, or any of the things that are waiting for them after class. Having a ritual that indicates the beginning of class and associating that beginning with a focus of attention will usually create a barrier between what was going on before and what is going on now.

Situation Two: *A student participates in class but frequently cuts in with jokes. While funny, this disrupts the concentration of other students and prevents the class from moving forward with any speed.*

This *may be* a problem if it frequently breaks the other students' concentration. The appropriate response to this depends on the context. It may help to let the class laugh. If you cut off all joy from the class, your students may perceive the class as being too strict. This student may be insecure about her performance. She may be using humor as a way of deflecting attention away from what she feels are her inadequacies. If you feel this is the case, you may wish to address the insecurities in private.

Perhaps it's better to ignore her comments and give them no attention. Lead the class and they will follow. If you show that the focus should remain on the lesson, others will do as you do. You may wish to address it in front of the class by saying something like, "All right, it's time to move on." You might also consider addressing it in private with a comment like, "It seems like you are having trouble focusing in class. Would you like to schedule a private lesson?" The point is to address it if it's disruptive. If this student is allowed to continue interfering with class, her behavior may set the standard that it's okay to laugh, joke, and talk throughout class. This can make it not easy for the instructor to maintain control.

Situation Three: *One of your students appears to either be intoxicated or suffering from a mental problem. She isn't able to concentrate and seems very spacey. She asks questions that you just answered. She comments on random topics that have nothing to do with class. Her movements are not very coordinated. She moves in opposition to the direction she is given. She reacts to correction as if you aren't talking to her or she responds by glaring at you.*

This is definitely a problem. It is not desirable to have this student in class. If she is intoxicated, she is sending the message that it's okay to be drunk or on drugs in class. This type of student makes others uncomfortable and can ruin any feeling of unity the class shares. If you have a policy about not using substances, you could use that as a means of dismissing her from class. If you cannot prove that the problem is due to intoxication, you can still dismiss the student on the grounds that her behavior is disruptive. It is better in the long run to dismiss one student than to risk the ruining the supportive learning atmosphere.

You may wish to talk to her first, but personality issues as strong as this are not usually resolved with a talk. My tactic would be to speak to her privately and start the conversation with something like, "It seems that this class is not a good fit for you. Perhaps you'd be happier learning with another group…" I would also offer her a refund for the unused portion of her tuition, because, although her behavior is disruptive, it doesn't appear to be intentionally so.

If you feel that it's best to deal with this with compassion and allow her to stay because belly dance is a therapeutic process that could help her, my advice is to leave that type of work to a trained therapist. This dancer has bigger issues than you are able to deal with in your classroom and it is not your job to "fix" her. Taking the time to do so could compromise your relationship with the rest of your students. I am not saying that you cannot allow her to stay in your class. I am just strongly advising against it.

Situation Four: *You have a talented student who is new to your area. Her previous teacher is someone whom she adores. As you are instructing, this student frequently cuts in with comments like, "We call that move this" or "We do that this way." She's very assertive and it comes across as if she is saying that you are doing things the wrong way.*

This is definitely a problem because talk like this could undermine your authority. If students perceive this student as a good dancer, they may believe you don't know what you are talking about if you don't address this in front of everyone. You do not want to get into a power struggle with anyone, so don't confront this with an authoritative attitude. You may wish to diffuse comments with responses like, "Yes, I know there is no set terminology, but in this class, that movement is called an undulation" and, "That's a legitimate move, but that's not what we are doing now." Her comments are most likely innocent. She's probably just anxious about being in a new situation and is missing her old teacher and friends. Give her a chance to get used to you and the new way of doing things, and she will probably come around. If not, talk to her in private about your perception of her behavior and try to come up with a plan for how to deal with it together.

Situation Five: *There has been a chaotic situation that affected many in your community (a hurricane, the death or serious illness of a beloved dancer, the arrest of a dancer, etc). When you enter the room, everyone is talking about what happened and is clearly not focused on class. You start class anyway, but it still remains obvious that their attention is elsewhere.*

This is not a problem. Sometimes it is appropriate to allow the focus to be on something other than dance for a while. Clearly this situation in the community is something that people need to talk about. Let them talk. This is an opportunity for supporting each other, learning about how they were affected, and growing closer together. Even though you aren't spending this time dancing, you are investing in your relationships and this is very valuable in creating feelings of belonging and caring. There will be times when cross talk and talk about our personal lives and situation is not only acceptable, but advisable. Feel it out.

I was in college when the terrorist attacks of September 11 happened. We spent days off topic talking about where we were and how we were coping. That time did nothing to further my education in counseling, but showing up was about all we could be expected to do. There was no concentrating on the lesson until we'd had a chance to feel normal again. It's up to you to judge when a situation should be jointly shared in class and how much time should be given to it.

Situation Six: *A student is very enthusiastic about "helping" others. She often goes over to other dancers and corrects them as you are in the front of the class teaching or giving someone personal attention.*

This may or may not be a problem. It really depends on the structure of your class and whether or not the student who is "helping" knows what she's talking about! If you are teaching a topic to mixed levels of students, it might be appropriate for those who are more advanced to lead those who are less advanced. For example, if you are teaching an improvisational tribal style to a mixed level group, it is easier to have helpers in the class if they know what they are doing. The helpers are developing leadership skills (which are needed to do tribal), and the followers are getting more individual attention.

If you are teaching a beginner level class and one person is or feels that she is quicker than the rest, it is not a good idea for her to be allowed to help others. The presumption is that everyone is at the same level. When one is allowed to stand out above the rest, it creates an atmosphere of favoritism. This is not productive. You want students to feel equally valued and held to the same standard. To allow a student of the same level to "help" others is not a good idea. If this student starts to do so, you could say something like, "Please direct your questions to me" or "Do you need some help back there?"

Managing your class isn't just dealing with undesirable behaviors. It's also about getting the desired behaviors to occur more often. To encourage appropriate behaviors (usually this refers to students executing movement correctly), you can nod, smile, or give a verbal affirmation like, "Yes, like that" or simply, "Very good." I had a teacher who gave out tassels to each student who completed a choreography. Tangible rewards are another way of reinforcing positive behavior, but I'd be careful about using these too often. The best rewards are intrinsic.

It may seem silly to talk about behavior management when most of our classes are filled with adults. Let's face it. Women can be full of drama. When you get together a bunch of ladies who like feeling pretty, talented, and special (and belly dance will do that for you!), they can get insecure, petty, and combative if they feel unsure of their status. The best way to diffuse that is to encourage mutual respect, give everyone the same type of attention, and address problems in a non-threatening way as soon as they arise.

It may seem that grown women don't need smiles and approval from you. They do. They are learning something new, and your approval matters a lot. So be liberal with praise and use criticism sparingly and constructively.

A well-managed classroom is a productive classroom. When students are happy and challenged, they keep coming back and they tell their friends. So, this is not just a good strategy for keeping things on an even keel. It's important to the longevity of your business. If you are not comfortable being the one in charge of other people's behavior, practice responses to potential situations.

It may sound silly, but practice makes a scary situation less frightening. It can give you courage and help you to deal with problems in a calm manner. If you have trouble manufacturing situations to practice, think back to situations that have happened when you were in class. Check online to see what students and teachers are talking about. Figure out a solution ahead of time so if it happens to you, you will be prepared for it. If you are uncomfortable giving praise, practice that. An effective teacher is adept at dealing with positive and negative behaviors.

Take a balanced approach to setting classroom norms. Don't be so strict that people feel uncomfortable asking questions. Questions are a gift. They allow you to see inside your student's head. Don't be so lax that there is continuous cross talk and progress can't be made on the lesson. Think before you act. Consider the impact of the behavior and your response to the behavior. This applies to both positive and negative behavior. If you compliment everything a dancer does, it leaves her little room to grow. If you correct every mistake, you may break her spirit.

How I Did It

I have given you my basic outline and lesson plans for my Foundations class. I used the Likert scale for evaluating progress. Students could score up to 2 points for each correct movement. The choreography, improv, and finger cymbal sections were worth 10 points each. Students had to score a 91% or better to pass. This meant that they had to pass the finger cymbals, improv, and choreography sections of the test. Students could test out whenever they were ready. I told them that it was rare to pass on the first try and let them know that they should test anyway because they would know exactly which movements they needed to work on to be more proficient. I felt that this took the pressure off being perfect.

This design developed over time. When I first started out, I taught a little bit of everything in each class. I found that it was not easy for students to retain that much information. I also found that students got bored with the same thing class after class. Once I broke it up into sections, the class started learning faster because we could spend more time on each section. They were able to remember movement better because we had more practice using the movements. They did not forget the things taught in previous classes because we frequently reviewed and used all movements in the free dance. The current design was slow enough for newcomers to keep up, yet challenging enough for students who had been there a while to remain interested.

Students who came in from other classes who truly were at an "intermediate level" could realistically test out within a month. That time was usually spent learning my vocabulary and a few new movements. Students who came in from other teachers with a beginning level of knowledge took as long to test out as the students who came in with no previous learning. This was usually because they were seeing things that were not taught in their other beginning level classes, and because they had to unlearn poor technique. It was realistic to expect a transfer beginner or new beginner who regularly attended class to test out within six months. Students who came to class on a casual basis and didn't rehearse on their own could take a year or longer to test out.

Once students tested out of Foundations, they went to "Beyond Basics." This class was ongoing. Each month we began a new topic of study. New students could begin at the start of the month only. In January we might focus on playing finger cymbals, then in February we could be doing tribal. At the start of each class, students were given a list of goals and objectives. They knew that they would be scored on how well they achieved those goals and objectives. The scores were given on a 5-point scale that was broken down like this:

1- did not demonstrate
2- sometimes demonstrated
3- adequately demonstrated
4- demonstrated well
5- demonstrated proficiently

Students were expected to achieve a 3, which basically said to me that they had a basic understanding of the concept, even if they had not yet mastered it. Nobody was expected to get a 5, which meant in my mind that they could teach the concept to others.

When I started the Beyond Basics class, students were given their assessments at the end of each month. As time went on, more and more students were not making 3's on their work. This was due to the lack of study time spent outside of class. Another reason for the lower than expected rates of proficiency was that those who started later did not get some of the more basic lessons that others before them had.

If I were teaching those classes today, I would start an intermediate session that would include classes in musicality, choreography, and improvisation that would be required before going into Beyond Basics, as the students who were not scoring well lacked that training.

Another thing I did was ask each student to write down their goals and when they wanted to achieve them. Periodically I would return their goals to them and ask them to look at them. If their goals had been met, I'd ask them to update their goals. If their goals had not been met, I'd ask them to think about whether or not the goal was still important or realistic. If it was, I'd ask what we could be doing to obtain it. I felt that this let the student know how far along she'd come. I also did this because I believe it focused their attention on the goal and made it more achievable.

Resources for Further Study

Books
Brandt, R. *Assessing Student Learning: New Rules, New Realities,* Educational Research Service, 1998. Print.

Seidel, K., *Assessing Student Learning: A Practical Guide (CD-rom),* Educational Research Service, 1998.

Websites
Creating Assessment Tool http://rubistar.4teachers.org

Framework for Ethical Decision Making
http://www.scu.edu/ethics.practicing/decision/framework.html

Lesson Planning http://www.adprima.com/lesosn.htm

Making Ethical Decisions
http://www.azcharacteredfoundation.org/ethical.html

National Dance Association http://www.aahperd.org

Before the Class Chapter Assessment

Design a class. This design should show:

- who is the target population of this class? (gender, age, skill level, etc)
- what is the subject of the class?
- are any pre-requisites required?
- is the class ongoing or in sessions? if sessions, how long is the session?
- what is the goal for the class?
- what are the objectives of the class?
- what tools are needed to teach this class?
- what is the time frame for completing your objectives?
- what level is the class geared to?

Include a written course description.

Include a lesson plan.

Create policies for this class.

Create an assessment tool for measuring whether your objectives were met.

The material should be formatted succinctly. It should be done in such a way that, if I had your vocabulary, I could come into your class with short notice and substitute for you, creating nearly the same class that you would if you were there.

Before the Class Chapter Assessment Results

Student name:_____ Date:_____

Items are scored on a 0-5 point scale. The goal is to achieve a 3, which means that you understand the material.

0- did not attempt
1- did not demonstrate a good understanding of the material
2- demonstrated some understanding of the material
3- demonstrated an understanding of the material
4- demonstrated good understanding of he material
5- demonstrated a mastery of the concept

___ Class description
___ Do the goals fit with the class description?
___ Can the goals be met with these objectives?
___ Does the class format work with the goals and objectives?
___ Do the tools used in class enhance the learning process?
___ Does the format allow adequate time to cover all the objectives?
___ Is the class material appropriate for the targeted audience?
___ Policies
___ Is the lesson plan written in such a way that the goals and objectives can be achieved in the time allowed?
___ Is the lesson plan clear and easy to follow?
___ Is the class outline created in such a way that I could substitute for this teacher with a moment's notice?
___ Does the assessment tool assess whether the goals and objectives were met?

Comments:

3 TEACHING METHODS

Goal: Students will be able to use a variety of teaching tools and methods.

Objectives:
- Students will be able to identify a student's communication style through observation
- Students will be able to teach using three different communication styles.
- Students will be able to use a variety of teaching tools
- Students will be able to use a variety of teaching methods
- Students will be able to discern a student's learning level
- Students will be able to teach to students with varying levels of skill
- Students will be able to critique students in such a way that encourages success
- Students will be able to critique their own performance to enhance effectiveness

Learning Styles

According to the neuro-linguistic programming (NLP) model, we experience the world through our five senses: sight, sound, touch, taste, and smell; however, we tend to favor one over the rest. People with a preference for visual communication get pictures in their head as they imagine things. They speak with "seeing" words such as:

How does this *look*?
I should keep *an eye* on that.
I *see* what you mean.
Did you *see* how she *looked* at me?
It *appears* that we are at an impasse.
I don't get it. *Show* me.
I really can't *picture* that.

They like doing visual things like watching sports or going to art museums. They are in tune with colors, shapes, and the way things look.

People with a preference for auditory communication connect with the way things sound. When asked to imagine things, they may hear things in their head. They speak with "sound" words like:

I like the way that *sounds*.
That guitar really *screams*.
Her *voice* is *shrill*.
I *hear* what you are saying.
That's a *booming sound* system.
Don't *shout* at me!
What I am trying to *say* is...

That *rings* a bell.

They like things like music and speaking.

People who prefer to communicate by kinesthetic means connect with how things feel. When asked to imagine something, they may connect with how it feels or the emotion surrounding it. They speak with touching words like:

I can't *grasp* that.
I have to follow my *gut*.
I need to get a *handle* on the details.
We are *solid* as a rock.
How could you be so *cold*?

Kinesthetic people like comfortable clothes. They may like to work with their hands and engage in contact sports. They may be intuitive and get a sense of things or people by how they feel.

There are so few people who communicate primarily through taste or smell that we will not discuss that.

There is another style however that is not exactly sensory based. It's auditory-digital. Auditory-digital people search for meaning and understanding. They lead with their intellect. Auditory-digital people like order, detail, facts, agendas, timelines, goals, skills, and routines. It's much easier to identify this type of person through her processes rather than her language though this person tends to use succinct, exact language.

Understanding the way someone processes information is invaluable if you want to communicate with them. Why? Picture this. You are an auditory person who is trying to communicate with a visual person. You keep telling your visual student, "Listen to the beat, follow the beat, and dance to the beat." You say, "DUH duh duh DUH, duh duh DUH..." to try to get her to find the accent, but she's just standing there completely puzzled. Is she stupid? No. She just has a hard time connecting with your auditory words when she processes information primarily through visual means. This is particularly true when dealing with new material. If you said, "Follow me," and allowed her to imitate your movement by watching you, you would be more successful because you are giving a visual person something to look at. Make sense?

So how do you bridge this gap? First you figure out what *your* dominant communication style is, then you figure out how to use other communication styles. Make a list of words associated with each communication style, then listen to how others use language. If you notice cues that are associated with one particular style, you can guess that that is their style. If you can switch to words that they use, you will have an easier time of connecting and understanding each other.

Let's practice identifying communication styles. Read over the following imaginary conversations and see if you can tell which modality each speaker prefers.

Example One
Jane: I'd really like to get a new car, but I am not sure what I am looking for. Can you show me what you've got?

Mark: Sure! Step right this way. I have a little baby that you will just love. Hop on in and see how it feels.

Jane: I don't know. It is easy on the eyes, but it appears that this is out of my price range.

Mark: Well, let's go inside and get a feel for what kind of financing we can arrange to get you on the road to being a new car owner.

Notice that Jane uses seeing words like: *show*, *eyes*, and *appears*, which indicates that she's probably visual. You may have noticed that Mark, on the other hand, uses touching words like *step*, *hop*, and *feel*. All those things are connected to how things feel. If this were a real scenario, my bet would be that Mark does not make the sale because he is not grasping what Jane is trying to say. These two have not made a connection.

Example Two
Lisa: Pat, you have really decorated this place so beautifully! It's so bright and colorful. I just love it!

Pat: Yeah, I was trying to tune into an ocean groove. Joe gave me a couple of options and that sounded the best to me.

Lisa: Well, you chose right. It looks amazing!

Pat: I know Joe will be singing my praises after this job. We really were on the same wavelength on this one.

Lisa is visual. She uses seeing words like: *beautifully, bright, colorful,* and *looks.* Pat is auditory. She uses words like *tune, sounded, singing,* and *"on the same wavelength."* While these two are not using the same communication style, neither is trying to teach or persuade, so it's not likely to end in a disagreement, misunderstanding, or missed opportunity.

So what do you do if you are trying to teach and notice that your student isn't following your communication style? Here is an example of how that might flow.

Example Three
Soraya demonstrates a figure eight, but she notices that a student is not able to follow her movements just by watching her. She continues moving in the same manner, but adds verbalizations saying, "One, two, three, and four.... Right hip to the right front. Right hip to the right back. Left hip to the left front. Left hip to the left back." Recognizing that this is also not getting the desired reaction, she changes her wording to, "Weight is on the right, weight is on the left." This gets some improvement, but not completely, so she finally goes over to her student, asks her permission to touch her, and guides the student's hips with her hands to the correct movement. This time it clicks!

In Example Three, Soraya first used a visual technique. Her words and body moved in the way that she was describing to help students approximate the same movement. When she saw that one student was not getting it, she switched to auditory technique. Auditory students will associate sound with movement. As long as the student is able to associate that sound with a movement, they will understand the general idea of what you are trying to get across. When that also failed to get a response, Soraya switched to a kinesthetic technique. She first tried getting the student to feel the weight shift in her body as the hips came off center to each side. Then she actually physically maneuvered the student's hips to get them to move in the desired direction.

Note: *When working with kinesthetic students, always ask before putting your hands on them. It is the respectful thing to do, and you never know if someone doesn't like being touched or equates touch with pain. This is also the culturally competent thing to do. Your verbalizations of where the student's weight should be are often enough to get them to feel it in their bodies without touch being necessary, so try that first.*

Another way to figure out a person's communication style is to look at the eyes. When NLP was first developing, early pioneers Bandler and Grinder observed that the way people move their eyes indicates which modality they are using.

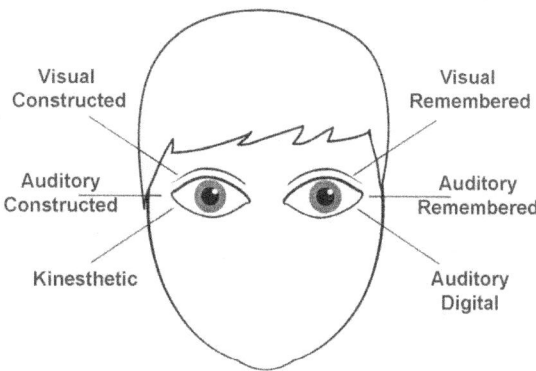

If you look at the picture above as if it were someone looking at you, you can see what the eyes of most people do when processing information. When asked, "What did you wear yesterday?" and the respondent visualizes what her clothes looked like, her eyes would go up and to the right (because it was in the past). If that same person were asked what she would wear tomorrow, her eyes would probably go up and to the left, because she's envisioning something that hasn't happened yet. (Incidentally, you can use this to get an indication if someone is lying. If the eyes go to the "imagined" position when they are formulating a response to a question, they are probably not being factual.) If you ask, "What did the music sound like?" the respondent's eyes would most likely go to the right. If they go down and to the right, they're hearing the music in their head.

If they were trying to imagine what something might sound like, the eyes would go to the left. Another way to remember this is, if the eyes move towards the ears, the person is trying to hear something.

If you ask someone what their new fur coat feels like, her eyes would probably go down and to the left as she is remembering the softness. This same thing is true for recalling how emotions feel. So the feeling can either be something that can be felt in the hands or simply felt through emotion.

For a person whose primary system is auditory digital, a question like, "Can you remember a poem from elementary school?" or "Can you recite the times tables to yourself?" could result in the eyes shifting down and to the left. They are accessing information from their internal dialogue.

If you would like to test this, here are some sample statements that you can have someone read to you or you can read to someone else. Document which way their eyes move (if at all) to see if the answer corresponds to the eye accessing cues. If the eyes remain straight ahead, that indicates a visual response to old or new information. Keep in mind that just as there are people who are left hand dominant, there are folks who switch right and left in eye accessing cues. So what most do to the right, they do to the left.

Test statements:

Think of what Santa Claus looks like.
Imagine what your next house will be like.
Notice the temperature of your fingers.
Hear the sound of a school bell.
Listen to the sound of an alien spaceship landing in your yard.

The best way to use this information while teaching is to get in the habit of teaching to all styles at once. Whenever you are speaking, you are using auditory technique. When you are moving in front of sighted people, you are using visual technique. If you just add verbal instruction that includes how the movement feels in the body, you will be teaching with all three modalities at once.

If you are having trouble figuring out a student's learning style fairly quickly, you may wish to give incoming students a questionnaire prior to starting class with you. The VARK Questionnaire can be found online at http://www.vark-learn.com.

Teaching Tools

<u>**Here are some tools for teaching to visual learners:**</u>

Video: I am strong visual learner. If I watch a video or a dancer's style often enough, I can imitate the movement without ever having walked through it or having to break it down. Visual learners are like this. Watching other students, video, and shows are great ways to show them how to incorporate movements, build upon things already learned, and create new movements.

"Follow the Leader": This is also called "follow the bouncing butt." Little to no auditory instruction is given, the students are primarily just following the instructor. This can be used for movements in isolation, combinations, drills, or choreographies. Any time you are leading a class to people who can see you, you are using visual teaching method.

Dry erase board: It often helps visual learners to see words associated with movements (or whole choreographies). Don't limit the board to words, however. If you are working on spacing, you can illustrate many configurations and have students follow the shapes written on the board. If you are teaching choreography, you can use this to create symbols for musical phrases like ~ for smooth, and //// for percussive. Don't be afraid to use a dry erase board or chalk board like a traditional classroom. Some traditional techniques work for dance too!

Flash cards: This is a variation of the dry erase board. Flash cards can be used to stimulate memory, drill movements, or test student's recall of movement and vocabulary.

Use of imagery: It can be very helpful to use imagery, especially when encountering a particularly challenging technique. Imagery allows you to bypass your critical mind (which isn't working) and step into your creativity. Imagery can be a visualization of something similar to what you want the body to do. For example, you could tell the student, "dance as if your body were a fluffy, white cloud, light and airy," to get a less heavy quality of movement. Imagery is not confined to what we can see. Shakira uses the question, "Where is your crayon?" to get students to experience how movement feels in the body when it originates in different places (which is kinesthetic imagery).

Here are some tools for teaching to auditory learners:

Singing: I often vocalize the music as we are learning the phrases. I sometimes will sing the words for movements to the tune of the music. Both techniques associate movement with music in the student's mind, so she can "hear" what comes next.

Vocalizations: This isn't exactly singing. This is just making sounds that give an idea of what the movement should be. For example, if I make a rolling sound with my tongue, that probably indicates a shimmying motion. If I make quick percussive sounds, I am probably looking for movements that start and stop suddenly, like a shoulder or hip accent. If my pitch is higher, that may indicate a movement that goes up in some way. The length of the sound may indicate the length of the phrase of movement.

Metronome: The metronome is a great tool students of any learning style can use to build speed with movements, but it is particularly good for auditory learners. The steady *tap, tap, tap* will help to keep them focused and on beat. Sometimes students will get distracted by all the things going on in the music and lose sight of the beat, making it a challenge for them to get the timing of combinations down. If you can practice them with a metronome, this often helps.

Clapping: Clapping out the beat can help auditory learners stay on tempo. This can help all students learn new rhythms.

Here are some tools for teaching to kinesthetic learners:

Use of feeling words: Feelings are invisible, so you have to rely mainly on words to reach kinesthetic learners through your voice. Instructions that focus on where the weight is, what body part is moving where, and what is touching something work well. Example, "Step right, step left; weight is on the right, weight is on the left; and flat, ball, ball, ball" (where the foot is on touching the floor with the full foot, and then on the ball).

Use of touch: Touch can be used to guide the student. It can also be a gentle touch on the shoulder or back to remind them of posture. Never force a student into a position. If the student is stiff and nervous, she is not likely to move very easily and that would be counter-productive. Leave it alone and correct it in another way at another time if you encounter this type of resistance.

This is the second least common learning style. If you have a student who struggles to learn and you are not kinesthetic, it is probably because she is.

Here are some tools for teaching to auditory digital learners:

Use lots of explanations: Auditory digital people want the world to make sense. It can seem that they can't move unless they have an understanding of what it is they are supposed to do and how it fits in the big scheme of things.

Link ideas together: Metaphors, concepts, maps, storytelling, and diagrams are ways to help things make more sense.

Allow them to move at their own pace: Auditory-digital people can appear slow to move until they feel comfortable. Let them ask questions. Let them get a feel for what is going on.

Most teachers use a "follow me" approach, at least through part of their class. Most teachers also speak during class. If you do those two things, you already use one visual and one auditory skill. The key to being more effective is to learn additional skills to reach all four learning modalities. People primarily use one method for processing information, but we have access to all four, so when one isn't working, try another one. Dance cannot be learned through one modality. However, because dance is a physical activity, many teachers use "doing" as the only teaching method. This creates a single dimension of learning in an art form that is truly multidimensional. When you learn to use tools that are visual, auditory, kinesthetic, and digital, it gives the student a much richer dance experience. Don't limit yourself to the tools included here. This is just a beginning. Explore and find other ways to use visual, auditory, kinesthetic, and digital ways of expressing movement.

Teaching Methods

There are many teaching methods used in dance. The most appropriate one will depend on your strengths and weaknesses, the focus of the class, the dance style, the students' level of skill, and many other variables. Having a variety of teaching methods will give you more flexibility to help students learn. It gives you "tricks" to try when the standard methods do not work. It keeps the class from being too predictable and boring.

Demonstration

The most commonly used method in belly dance is demonstration. The teacher executes a movement or combination and the class follows. This is a great way to teach dance. If the instructor is giving direction as she moves, this technique uses visual, auditory, and kinesthetic modalities. The student observes. She listens to the instruction. Then she executes it with her own body. When the teaching method reaches out with visual, auditory, *and* kinesthetic modalities, the student is more likely to understand the material and retain it.

Homework

I am very discouraged by the lack of focused practice among belly dance students. Students who came to me from other dance forms often said, "You only teach twice a week?" They were used to taking dance lessons more frequently and rehearsing every day. This type of dedication is rare among belly dancers, and it should be encouraged. Practicing outside of class is an essential part of growth in any activity.

You can set the tone by ending each class with homework. For example, when I was teaching a specific style, the overall goal was for the students to know it when they saw it and be able to execute rudimentary movements in that style. The first class could be on music. The students would listen to music that was indicative of that style. We might explore the rhythms and play with how they felt. We might also look at video and pictures so that they would know how the style is costumed. The homework for that class would be to find music in that genre and listen to it. In the next class, we would work on movements and stylization that is typical for that dance style. The goal was to get the feeling in our bodies. They would be expected to work on that, so that when we got to the next class, which was a short choreography, they would have some understanding of how it would all fit together. During the last class, the students would put together a choreography or improvisation of the dance style. Without rehearsal in between, the students would drop out of class because they'd be too overwhelmed.

Assigning homework sets the expectation that students will approach dance with discipline. It helps them to become aware of their strengths and weaknesses. It also builds their muscle memory.

If you teach a class for self-esteem, don't dismiss the idea of homework, thinking that it doesn't apply to you. Just because the class is fun doesn't mean that the students can't benefit from homework. The goal of homework could simply be to work up to dancing to a three-minute song. Perhaps they could benefit from seeing how many ways they can do a hip circle. Keep an open mind about the level of difficulty. Rehearsal doesn't have to be approached like it is work.

Problem-Solving

Problem-solving means giving the student a question or task to which she has to find the answer. The homework example above is a problem-solving task. In the end, the student is solving the "problem" of interpreting what a certain style looks like. At the end of that class, she should know how the style is costumed, what music goes along with it, and how to recognize and execute stylistic movements associated with that genre.

Problem-solving is a fantastic teaching method because it gives the student freedom to express herself. She becomes free from the teacher's structure and can explore things on her own. She has to make choices about what to accept or disregard. She puts all of her learning to work for her, which expands her knowledge.

Although this sounds like a method that is suitable for intermediate to advanced students, this can be used for beginners as well. Just keep the "problem" simple. It could be something as easy as, "How can you dance for an entire song using only a grapevine, shimmy, snake arms, and an undulation?" This problem only requires that the dancer know four movements and use a little creativity.

Collaboration

Collaborate means to work together. Students learn a lot from each other. If you are doing all the teaching all the time, you are working way too hard! Take a break. When the students work together, it gives them the opportunity to learn things in new ways. They may say something in a different way than you do that clicks with their fellow students. They may make up a new way of doing things that is easier. They may make mistakes that lead to jumping off points for new ideas. All kinds of things can happen when the attention moves from the instructor to the students.

Although this is a great teaching method, it's not advisable for all classrooms. This works best when the students know and trust each other, have roughly the same level of skill, and are not afraid to work in front of other people.

One way I used collaboration in the classroom was to have the students show their works in progress to the rest of the class. The performer had to be open to feedback. The "audience" had to be respectful and give both positive and negative feedback. This gave the performer an opportunity to have her work viewed by more than just my two eyes. She usually got subjective and objective comments. This helped her to look at subjective and objective things from various points of view. This experience helped both the performer and the audience. Although the audience members weren't dancing, they could see how others reacted to the performance and use that feedback for their own performances.

Another way I used collaboration was in improvisational tribal. I often had people pair up with others to work on transitions and duets. I liked to pair strong leaders with weak followers. This tended to make both partners strong because they had to pay closer attention to each other. In both examples of collaboration, the students were able to process the exercise and what worked or didn't work for them.

A third example of collaboration is to divide the class in half. Have one half dance while the other half watches. When the dancers are finished, allow the watchers to comment on what they saw. Then have the watchers dance and the dancers comment. This experience gives dancers a way to learn that can't occur simply through dancing. It's very difficult to see what's going on on stage when you are the one on stage. Even with mirrors, it's a different experience from sitting still and being an observer.

As I think back on my primary instructors, I realize that every single one of them only used demonstration as a means of instruction. While I think that this is probably the *best* technique, it is certainly not the only one. When people complain that they have to do choreography and/or combinations in beginner classes because the class will be bored otherwise, I have to disagree. There are no boring classes, just boring teachers. I think it's much better to work with basics for as long as it takes the student to master them, than to throw more advanced material at students who aren't ready for it. If you teach with variety, challenge the students with homework, play, experiment, and collaborate, your students will always be entertained as they learn.

How Students Learn

As someone who spent three years of undergraduate study as a psychology major, I can tell you that there are many theories about how people learn. Some of these have been challenged recently, and few have related to how people learn dance, but the thing that most have in common is that learning progresses from the simple to the complex.

First Level Learners

When Leila dances, she looks like she is counting or maybe thinking. She has that little hesitation at the end of an eight-count phrase before moving on to the next thing. Her arms are close to her body as if to say she's not quite comfortable with them. When traveling, her feet seem to arrive half a second behind the rest of her. Her timing is usually on, but when she gets off, she has to start at the beginning of the dance phrase to catch up. Leila is a first level learner.

When teaching new students or new techniques, remember that some students will not be able to access more than one learning modality at a time. This means when teaching something new, you may wish to tell the student what you are going to do, then execute the movement before asking them to do it. This goes along with the first stage of learning, in which students visually identify movements, relate them to vocabulary, and execute the movements with limited ability. It is important at this stage of learning to provide lots of review so that information can be retained. This means repeating your movements and repeating your instructions over and over.

Instructors should use a variety of techniques to reach students of all learning styles and reinforce learning on different levels. Instructions should be clear, simple, and broken down into manageable parts. Feedback should encourage students, identify errors, and correct problems in a neutral to positive way. Remember that student may revert back to this level whenever presented with new material, so you may have to slow down when presenting brand new material, even for advanced level students.

A student in the first stage of learning may start a basic movement in the same place every time. She may have to think about the name of the movement for a moment before she can execute it. Her movements may not be crisp and clean. The parts of the movement may not be visible and the movement may not flow seamlessly.

When working with students at this level, it is appropriate to give them material that they can execute. Whole choreographies, long combinations, and layers are not appropriate for beginning dancers at this level. Although it is not impossible for beginners to learn these things, it takes away from the solid development of core skills and may disguise their lack of ability. It is much harder to undo poor technique than it is to teach good basics, so teaching choreographies, long combinations, and layers to beginners is ill advised.

For example, I inherited a student who had been taking lessons for about six months. When she came to my class, she had horrible figure eights. We spent a lot of time breaking the movement down. I worked with her over a year. She could do it correctly when I was standing there instructing her through it, but reverted back to her old habits when she was dancing. So at the end of her time with me, she still had the same horrible figure eights. Why? Because it's harder to overcome poor technique than to teach it correctly the first time. Please do yourself and your students a favor and correct poor technique. Review a lot. Give them instruction in a variety of modalities. Help them get the proper movement vocabulary imbedded into their muscle memory from the start.

When teachers give students a lot of material in a beginner class, it's more likely that the student will "cheat" and get by on movements that are somewhat correct. This is not a good way to develop strong students, because as more vocabulary is added, the mistakes become compounded. I've heard teachers argue that students get bored if they don't have something more than basics. It doesn't matter if your class is technique-focused or stress relief-focused. You can find ways to be creative while giving students movements that they can successfully execute.

Examples of exercises that use beginner level movements:

1) Practice movements in isolation

2) Use only traveling steps to give students a chance to explore movement in space. They could move for eight counts, stay still for eight counts, and repeat while making patterns in space (diamond, square, circle, etc.)

3) Partner dance. Each student faces another. They have to attempt to move in different ways from their partner. So if one is using her arms above her head, the other may focus on filling the space below the navel. If one is doing smooth moves, the other could be doing percussive moves.

4) Explore qualities of movement. Throw out words and have the students interpret them using belly dance moves. For example: chocolate, morning, birth, driving, kindergarten, etc.

5) "Simon says." Play belly dance Simon Says. This tests the student's name recognition of movements in a playful way.

While teaching at the first stage of learning, teachers may incorporate arms and feet into the class, but do not expect a fine degree of control of the extremities. Students at this level will learn to control the center of the body first, then the extremities, then the head. The more that you give the student to accomplish, the longer it will take her to master the basics. This is not to say that you should not use frames, layers, or combinations. This is just to let you know that you should allow time for the learning process to take place when planning how much material to put into each session.

Think of it this way. Have you ever been in a ballet class? What about tap? If you have, you will know that beginner level classes spend a lot of time repeating very basic movements in isolation. This isn't to bore the student, but to build skill and correct muscle memory. Even when arm movements are added, they are very simple movements that focus on precision execution. I realize that belly dance is not ballet, but good teaching technique crosses the boundaries of the art form.

Make an informed decision when introducing material in class that is more advanced than the students at a particular level. If it makes sense to do it, do it. When I first started dancing, my first two teachers did nothing with arms. Once I was proficient with basic movements, it was like starting all over trying to figure out what to do with my arms. Had I had that as a beginner, all I would have had to do was refine my movements rather than start from scratch.

As an instructor, I know that students will not have much awareness of their arms in the beginning, but I make them frame movements anyway. This is my own personal call, based on my experience as a student. When you do things that do not fit within the learning model, be able to justify it and make allowances with the amount of time it will take to accommodate the material that is more advanced than the students are.

Also modify it so that students are not expected to execute intermediate level movements at the beginner level. Remember to give them material that they can successfully execute. The beginning learner may be very intimidated by being in a classroom. Take this into consideration when asking her to do things (like dancing in front of the class alone). The new student's ego may be fragile, so if she wants to dance in the back or not participate, take notice of that. She may need time and encouragement before she is emotionally strong enough to fully participate. Nurture this, because a student who does not participate is very limited in what she can achieve.

You can encourage participation by pausing in your verbal instruction to give students a chance to ask questions. Ask your students to share their questions in class so that others may benefit from the answers, but be available before and after class for questions, too. Ask students questions to determine their level of understanding. Use them as a resource, if it's appropriate. Call on students by name. If you make questions a normal part of class, it will encourage shy students to speak up and join the class.

Second Level Learning

Gamilla follows along well. She picks up material quickly and is able to incorporate it into her rehearsal and performances. She is often able to think through her own questions and figure them out for herself. She's recently become aware of how her feet look and is working on always keeping them pointed nicely. She is also refining her hand movements. She's lost that "dead energy" look in her hands. Her frames are not just framing her movements. They are movements in themselves. Gamilla is a second level learner.

The second stage of learning relies on fewer cues and less verbal instruction. It focuses on nuances, variations, transitions, musicality, and artistry. Review is important to retain technical ability. Movements are varied in time (full time, half time, and quarter time) and space (in place, while moving side to side, or with a height change). Movements are combined differently to create new combinations and new ways of using old steps. Mental practice is encouraged. (Studies show that students who do mental rehearsal are as proficient or more so than those who engage solely in physical rehearsal). Students should be able to self-correct and become more responsible for their progress. Feedback is targeted and given less often to encourage self-correction.

Students at this level of learning can be identified by their ability to dance short combinations (3-4 steps). Their technical ability is more solid. They can coordinate the hands and feet with the body. Their sense of timing is more acute. The quality of movement is more musical and emotional.

Instruction at this level should focus on developing these skills. Choreography can be introduced. Improvisation should certainly be used. Visual exercises in being and becoming the music are encouraged. Drills can be incorporated for review purposes and to keep the technique up to par. Drills should make use of a change in timing, change in dynamics, and a change in the order of movements to create new combinations.

Instruction at this level should also encourage analytical thinking. When a question is posed, see if the student can answer it herself. Ask other students their opinions on the topic, if it's appropriate. A student in the second level of learning often only needs guidance to answer her own questions, because she already has a large knowledge base. Teaching students to think critically greatly expands their ability to apply what they already know and expand it in ways that overlaps other subjects.

Third Level Learning

Delilah rehearses to the same song over and over. She watches herself intently in the mirror, trying on new faces, playing with the mood of the piece. She makes subtle changes, but can tell when they have made a little improvement. She sometimes stumbles on new combinations through her "play." It just comes out of her and seems like the right thing to do at the time. When that happens, she rehearses it over and over until she feels she won't lose it. Delilah is a third level learner.

In the third stage of learning, the instructor demonstrates less and uses fewer vocal instructions, as the dancer can now perform movements, phrases, and choreographies accurately and without thinking about them. The exception to this is when the instructor is taking a seemingly simple concept and studying the subtleties or depths of it. The instructor's goal here is more to guide the development, encourage confidence, and correct technique.

Students at this level can be determined by their ability to execute movement seamlessly and without thinking about it. This gives them the freedom to concentrate on style, personality, presentation, and emotional quality. Movements are habitually correct. Performances are more artistic and meaningful.

Instruction at this level should be focused on diversifying technical ability (adding dynamics, creating new combinations and frames), developing artistry, and expanding knowledge of styles. Choreographies can be more complex. Improvisation should now flow because the dancer is expected to have an innate understanding of the music. Drills are never abandoned. Exercises to enhance the expression and understanding of space should be used.

Matching Teaching Methods and Learning Levels

You can tell where a student is in her mastery of any given technique by looking at how she attacks it. If she is lacking in control of her extremities, you can guess that she is at the first level of learning—at least for that particular technique. So your teaching should be focused on what a first level student can accomplish. When your instruction is targeted to the specific learning level of the student, you are more likely to get success.

This information is also important to know so that you classify your classes correctly. Classes should be labeled based on the type of learning that takes place within the class. If every movement needs to be broken down and students require a high degree of correction for movements in the body rather than the extremities, you have a beginner class and it should be labeled as such.

If you have students who can execute combinations, layers, and choreographies, and are able to self-correct, you have students in the second level of learning (or intermediate level students). You should not be teaching to them using first level techniques (which is what I most often see at all levels). Your teaching methods should be parallel to *their* learning level.

If your students are focusing on emotional quality, broadening and deepening their level of technical expertise, and can often answer their own questions, they are advanced. Your role should be to guide development, provoke analytical thought, and help them to put concepts together to increase knowledge. Be sure to properly label this class.

If all instructors had properly labeled classes, it would create consistency. The label for a class should not be determined by the number of classes that the student has taken or the number of years she has studied, but by her proficiency at dance and the level of instruction that she requires to continue growing. The techniques for teaching different levels of learners are not the same.

Understanding levels of learning and how to teach to students at different levels is also beneficial for *your* growth. If you know what type of rehearsal and break down that you need, you can create personal workouts that are most beneficial for your growth. If you practice using only basic level techniques, your skill will never grow beyond a basic level. If you teach using only basic level techniques, your students will either become bored and leave you, or they will remain beginner level students.

Before I leave this topic, I want to add that knowing your students' level can help you anticipate transition and termination before it happens. You should expect your students to leave at some point. It's part of the growth process.

Think about it like a parent/child relationship. The job of the parent, from birth to adolescence, is to prepare the child for independence. As the adolescent learns more, she becomes more rebellious. She tries things that may be different from the parent's values. She is learning how to become her own person. This can be a time of strengthening ties or a time of strife. It all depends on how it is handled.

The fledgling dancer does the same thing. As she becomes more certain of her technique and expression, she may feel that she needs her teacher less. She may start exploring different styles or developing her own style within a style. Transition is a healthy and normal part of development. If you meet this with resistance, this dancer may break with you. If you meet it with support and appreciate it for what it is, your relationship can continue to be a good one, whether the dancer breaks from you or not.

In counseling (I am a professional counselor in my "other life"), we always say that you prepare the client for termination from the first meeting. The same should be true of dance teachers. When you know that there will be a point at which you can no longer be of service to your student, it's easier to accept that they will either move on to another teacher or become teachers themselves. Mentally prepare for that and see any pulling away for what it is. Don't take it personally.

Cognitive Stages of Learning

Another way to determine what level of proficiency a student has is to look at this is through Abraham Maslow's stages of learning. The first stage is Unconscious Incompetence. In this stage, the student doesn't know what she doesn't know. The teacher's job here is to be very directive to develop skill, passion, and respect for the art form, while keeping in mind that the student has little ability for refinement. Instruction should be focused on basic, foundational skills.

Maslow's second stage of learning, Conscious Incompetence, is when the student realizes she's not proficient, finds it challenging to be as good as she'd like to be, but doesn't know how to reach her goals. The instruction at this stage should continue to be directive, concrete, and contain a lot of constructive feedback. Let the student know what was done well and what needs to be changed. This will help prepare her for the next level of learning.

The third stage is Conscious Competence. At this level, the student knows what she has to do to become better and has the skills to achieve it, but she has to think about it. This is a working stage in which the movement requires thought and still feels contrived. At this stage, the instructor's role becomes more facilitative. She is less directive and more reflective. Reflective tasks are about helping the student to think for herself. Open ended questions, group discussion, exploring options, and seeking creativity are reflective forms of teaching.

The last stage is Unconscious Incompetence. At this level, movement, artistry, and technique flow flawlessly without thought. The student takes primary responsibility for her learning. The instructor's role is largely supportive. She may help creativity to blossom and encourage the dancer to grow in new directions.

I have seen natural dancers who are able to do this without ever having passed through a stage of feeling unsure of themselves, but this is rare. If you want to create students who are thinkers, can make informed choices, teach others, and continue to grow, it's best to allow them to flow through all steps and change your role to become directive and more reflective as they move through each stage. You will get more consistent results this way.

Types of Learning

Enculturation. Enculturation refers to learning things that are a part of the natural environment. In dance, this doesn't usually refer to movement, but it does include things like what to wear to a class, performance etiquette, classroom behavior, etc.

Observation. It is often said that people are role models. What this means is that they are visible, so their behavior can be copied. There isn't any plan in place to have the behavior copied. It just happens through observation. This is another way that people learn. To apply this to the classroom, new teachers with no formal teaching training usually teach the same way that their teachers taught. They learned this through observation.

Play. Play is an activity that is meant to be enjoyable and has no particular goal. This is an excellent way to learn, because the benefits of the activity are usually generalized to other things. For example, let's look at the Layers game. The dancers stand in a circle. The instructor starts off the game by doing a move, let's say a hip circle. The person to the right can either add or subtract a move. Since she's the first one, she can only add because if she stopped doing the hip circle, there would be no movement, so she adds a shimmy. They are now doing a hip circle with a shimmy. Play passes to the next person and that person adds or subtracts. The game doesn't rely on each person being able to do a hip circle with a shimmy overlay, but it presents the idea that it may or may not be possible (all combinations won't work well). Having engaged in this exercise, the dancer may broaden her repertoire by adding new moves or by simply having a way to create new moves that she's never seen before.

Reinforcement. When a behavior occurs and is followed by positive reinforcement, it is more likely that the behavior will be repeated. For example, if you throw a stick and a dog brings it back to you (behavior), then you pet him and tell him he's a good boy (positive reinforcement), it is more likely that the dog will do it again—assuming the dog likes you and wants to be petted by you. If a student does a movement correctly (behavior) and you smile (positive reinforcement), she is more likely to do that movement correctly again.

Rote. Rote is the introduction of material that is learned by repetition. You may have seen examples of this in old or period movies, in which third graders are reciting *Charge of the Light Brigade* or where foreign students are repeating phrases in English like, "breakfast… lunch… dinner…" A dance example of this is teaching beginners choreography. It focuses on being able to repeat exactly what was presented, but doesn't address the nuances, concepts, or inter-relational ideas of the elements of dance. This makes it less likely that the student will be able to break down ideas and apply them to other situations. However, this may be appropriate in some circumstances, such as when you are making a study of a certain choreographer's style.

Tangential. Tangential learning is being able to pick up something that wasn't specifically taught by taking what you already know and applying it elsewhere. If you do a good job of breaking down elements and exploring them in isolation, your students are more likely to engage in tangential learning. An example of this is taking a combination out of a choreography and using it in improvisation. Another example would be taking a layered move that you learned in class and adding a height and directional change to it, making a unique move. A third example would be learning one specific style through choreography and using that as the basis to create a new choreography in the same style.

The goal for a good teacher is to use the most effective techniques to achieve the goal in mind. My overall goal for teaching is that my students learn to be the best dancers they are capable of being, given their available time, interest level, and natural aptitude. With that in mind, I am always breaking down and exploring elements of dance, so that they can be expressed in ways that are technically correct and uniquely their own. So rote learning is seldom seen in my classes. The culture of my classroom is respectful and professional, so that we all take things seriously and the classroom is a safe place to learn. I use a lot of positive reinforcement. When I give criticism, it is targeted to the problem and a solution is offered. Reinforcement in terms of reviewing the same types of material over and over is also used heavily. For example, all dance is taught with musicality in mind, from the first class onward, so it's not likely that a student will dance in ways that are not musical. Despite the professional atmosphere, play is also heavily used. We call them "exercises," but they are open-ended exercises with the goal of exploration and creativity in mind.

When you keep in mind all the ways you can teach, who you are teaching to, the goal of the class, and what you can accomplish with your lesson plan, you are more likely to get the result you want. Your students won't be bored because you have endless possibilities. And your students will learn quickly and much more than they would if you just taught moves in isolation, combinations, and choreographies. Think like a western dance teacher. That is not what they do. They learn how to teach and spend time developing the dancer, not the dance.

Teaching to Different Levels in the Same Classroom

It is common in belly dance to have students in the same class who are not of the same skill level. It is even more common at the workshop level, so instructors have to be well informed about how to teach to different levels and different learning styles at the same time. You may wish to separate the class into two sides of the room or two groups. Have the lower level class do the simpler technique, while asking the more advanced level to execute a more advanced version of the same thing. Here are some examples:

Simple	**More Complex**
grapevine	grapevine with a shimmy overlay
shimmy	shimmy at twice the speed
3/4 shimmy	3/4 shimmy while walking
karsilama step	karsilama step while turning to the corners
3/4 shimmy walk	3/4 shimmy walk on the ball
repeat the combination	add new combination the 2nd time
hip drop add arms	hip drop ask student to point her feet
movement without emotion	movement with emotion

Whether you need to simplify the class or make the class more complex, you can do this by adding or subtracting technique, as shown above. Changing the timing, going up on the ball or taking it to flat footed, adding or subtracting a layer, or walking or turning with a step can change the level of complexity. The same can be done when teaching choreographies.

The "danger" of having two levels of students in the class is that the slower students may want to do the tougher technique, rather than focusing on mastering their own. You want your students to stretch themselves, but you also want them to be able to execute everything cleanly, so be sure to give students feedback. If they feel challenged doing the lower level material, they will most likely stay there. The atmosphere of the class must also be supportive, so that they do not feel they are in competition with anyone or feel that they stand out in a negative way if they aren't able to do the harder movements.

Another way to challenge the more advanced student is to have her focus on the emotional quality of the piece. Beginners will struggle with just getting the mechanics down, but an intermediate or advanced level student can play with it to see how she wants to express it. If you do this, the beginner will be less likely to imitate the more advanced students.

As your students progress, your role should move from being in front of the class, dancing every step, and guiding the students' progress to observing more, walking around the room, giving individual correction, and allowing the student to self-correct. Intermediate and advanced students should be able to tell when they are not getting it right. They should be able to build on skills learned previously to figure out what to do next. If you use a variety of teaching tools and teach technique from simple to complex, you shouldn't have to demonstrate and dance with the class from start to finish. Unless circumstances demand it, I would not recommend having regular weekly classes with students of different levels (beginner/intermediate) in the same class. Their needs are very different. However, workshop situations will almost always demand that you have the ability to teach to drastically different levels of students in the same classroom, so practice this skill.

Putting It All Together

In the first chapter, we talked about creating lesson plans. We reviewed how there should be an overall goal and objectives to help you get there. As I have said before, I have observed that many teachers teach using the same techniques and same exercises for all levels of learners. This is not the most effective way to teach.

Remember when you were a first grader learning how to spell? You practiced writing big letters all by themselves. Then you put letters together to make simple words like cat and dog. Then your letters got smaller and your writing became smoother and easier. Right? Now imagine that you are in second grade. You already know how to write and read a little, but your teacher teaches using the same techniques that your first grade teacher used. Can you see how you might not be challenged because you have already mastered that? Can you see how your education might be stunted? Knowing how students learn can make sure that you do not do this as a dance teacher.

So let's say that I am teaching a workshop on sword with different levels of learners. Some are coming to their first workshop ever. Some have danced a bit, but this is their first encounter with sword. Some have been dancing a long time and have danced with the sword before. Here is how I could create my lesson plan.

Goal: Each student will leave the workshops with tips and tricks on how to use the sword in a performance.

Objectives:
Students will have a basic understanding of sword safety and handling.
Students will learn many balancing points typically used in sword dancing.
Students will have a complete choreography to use as an example of a completed sword routine.

Note that my objectives for the mixed level class are the same for all levels in this example, but this does not need to be the case. What will make this a suitable class for all levels is how I go about executing my plan.

My plan for the whole class starts with the first two objectives. First, I would talk about how to safely handle the sword to avoid cutting yourself or having it fly off into the audience, and making sure it stays securely on your head—as much as it possibly can—while maintaining the illusion that it's a sharp and dangerous object. If you don't create the illusion that it's dangerous, there is no suspense or mystery in the performance. Next, I go over the "tricky" balancing points that are used in the choreography, including the transitions of how to get the sword into position and how to get it gracefully back into your hands. If there are precise musical counts, we will review the movement over and over to get the timing down correctly.

This will be targeted to the different levels through the execution and difficulty level of the choreography, which comes next. For my beginners, I will give them the most repetitive version that has fewer layers and shorter combinations. For my intermediates, I will give them less repetition, more layers, and longer combinations, if it makes sense musically to do this. I won't add difficulty for the sake of being technical or challenging. For my more advanced dancers, I will ask them to focus on the audience contact, expressive elements, and perhaps take the slower, taxim parts and make them juicy.

Ultimately, I would hope that all levels of students could be able to handle the sword smoothly and safely, know enough about how and where to balance that they could incorporate that knowledge into their own routines, and have enough of an understanding of the choreography that they could execute it with additional practice and use it as a template to construct their own piece. (Those are my objectives). I would also hope that beginners could put the moves together, that intermediates could execute it with feeling and a higher level of technique, and the advanced students could make it their own. Why? Because that would be a reflection of their level. If you don't challenge students to live up to their level, they often will just do what you tell them to do and underachieve.

Moving To The Next Level and Beyond

But let's say that you have been teaching the same way all this time at a beginner level and don't know what to do to get your students to the next level. You've done movements in isolation. You have done combinations and drills and maybe even some choreography. What then?

Basic movement is the foundation of everything. It's always good to start there, because it's the one thing we all have in common. I like doing exercises with intermediate level dancers because it gets them thinking about things in different ways and invites creativity. So playing games with basic movement is a good way to expand understanding. The Layers game mentioned earlier is an example of an intermediate level game.

Another exercise could be to explore qualities of movement. You split your class up into three groups: smooth, percussive, and travel. Take a piece of music that the class is familiar with and have them dance it ONLY WHEN THEIR DESIGNATED SOUND IS PLAYING. So, the smooth group can only dance smooth movements to smooth sounds. When that music segues into something else, they stop and the next group dances. What you should see is that there is some overlap in sounds and most music isn't all smooth, all percussive, or all travel. If you let each group dance to each part of the music, you should have a lot of feedback on how the music led the dancing, how the interpretation changed, and how the way they heard the music changed, as well as countless other ideas. The participation, observation, and discussion should create a level of learning that can't be achieved by drilling moves in isolation, combination, or doing whole choreographies.

This type of instruction is far more targeted to intermediate level learners than doing a new choreography each session. Choreography is a great learning tool, but if that is the only tool or primary tool in your toolbox, you and your students are missing out on the subtleties of dance that move a student from being a decent dancer to a great one.

Do you get the impression I want you to go outside of the drill – choreography- drill box? I do. Unfortunately, folk dances are often taught by untrained hobbyists who don't think they require the same level of education and thought used by established stage dances. I think that this is one of the things that keeps us stepsisters in the dance world. More importantly, I think that this is what keeps our students from achieving their full potential and keeps us from having the thriving studios that are possible. So create lesson plans for the level of students that you have. Challenge them. Help them to develop their ability to self-critique. Help them to continue their growth.

Critiquing the Student

In order for students to improve, they have to be critiqued. Critique includes praise, constructive criticism, and instruction for how to improve.

All students of any subject respond to praise. Always make use of praise, but tailor your responses to the goals of the class. If the goals are to increase self-esteem, relieve stress, or get in touch with femininity or spirituality, there can almost never be too much praise. Praise approximations of success as well as actual success. Praise effort. Praise expression. The point is to encourage and keep the student moving toward the goal. Dance is the tool for achieving the goal, so technique should not be the focus of the critique.

If your class is focused on learning dance and improving dance skills, praise effort if the student is struggling. Praise achievement when she accomplishes the goal. If there is nothing positive to say, you can either give some words of encouragement ("Keep trying, you'll get it") or don't say anything.

The amount of constructive criticism and its delivery is influenced by the goals of the class as well. For a self-esteem class, the ratio of praise to criticism should be at least three to one. If you are teaching a technique-based class, it is important to balance praise and criticism too, but this does not necessarily mean that you should give a positive comment to every negative one. That may come across as insincere. Just be on the lookout for things to praise. Comment favorably when there is something to comment on. Be fair.

If you give praise when it is warranted and criticism when it is deserved, your students will respect your assessment and listen to you. They will gain self-esteem from your praise, because they will know it is deserved. They will have a realistic sense of their ability because you tell them what is good and what needs work. They will also learn how to self-critique, which can mean the difference between developing a good dancer and a great dancer.

Never deliver criticism in a way that is hurtful, unproductive, personal, discriminatory, or disrespectful. Feedback should be delivered globally first. Most students have problems with the same things when they are learning new things, so this shouldn't be hard to do. Most of the class should respond to the correction by making a change. If a student does not make the change, restate the correction using a different learning modality (visual, auditory, kinesthetic). If this does not result in a change, address the students individually.

Another way to address the class globally is to ask one or two students who are correctly interpreting your instructions to demonstrate for the class. (Be careful not to choose the "best" students all the time, so that you avoid creating a teacher's pet or the perception of favoritism.) Use these models to point out the correct execution of the movement.

Feedback doesn't have to be strictly verbal. You can give encouragement by nodding your head. You can touch someone on the shoulder blades to remind them to keep from pinching their shoulder blades together. You can guide the body with your hands to manipulate the student into the correct movement. Be sure to use a broad range of techniques in giving feedback to maximize communication.

Do not give negative feedback on someone's movement or expression without giving them specific feedback on how to improve. If the movement is incorrect, explain why and tell them what you want them to do differently. If you are teaching something specific, like emotional quality, and they are going for a sensual look and it comes across looking painful (which is pretty common), tell them why the look is not consistent with their vision and give specific things to try that will change the emotional quality. Have them try it out in front of you and see if you get the change.

Things like this are subjective, so ask others in the class for feedback on this if the class atmosphere has the appropriate level of trust. If you treat every student fairly, they should have no problem giving and receiving honest feedback. If your student is supposed to be doing a particular style and has the nuances of the style wrong, explain why she's not capturing the style. Give visual examples of how she could improve. Show her what you want to see and explain why your example is more on the mark than hers.

Students learn and become more confident when they understand the whys. As they grow, they can take that information and apply it to other dance situations, so that their dance knowledge grows and they do not have to make the same mistakes over and over. When given specific feedback, students learn to self-correct. It isn't until a student has the ability to self-correct and gets targeted feedback than she can truly begin to grow and explore her own style. So give your students that gift.

Criticism is not a bad thing. It's a tool for growth. When it's delivered honestly, consistently, with praise, and with instructions for what to do differently, it is the best tool you have for sharing your knowledge and creating good dancers. Conversely, when you praise everything, you give your students a false sense of their level of ability, and they may never develop the balanced attitude to hear and appreciate constructive criticism that can make them better.

If your student is not responding to your feedback, change your approach. It may be helpful to switch to a different communication method. You may have to exaggerate what she's doing, then follow that with the desired movement so that she can see it. You may want to ask her to do it the wrong way followed by the right way, so that she can feel the difference in her body. Don't give up. It's not that the student is being passive aggressive or doesn't want to get it. It's just that she doesn't understand what to do differently.

Before I leave the topic of critiquing students, I want to reiterate the importance of *how you critique* because I strongly believe that it is one of my secrets of success. As a counselor, I have a low number of clients who terminate treatment prematurely—in fact, many want to stay after their issues have been resolved! My results are often quick and long lasting. I bring this up because I believe that my successful counseling techniques are the same skills used to make my teaching so successful.

So what's the secret? The secret is in the relationship with the instructor. Teachers who provide a safe, supportive atmosphere where students can openly express themselves and explore through dance are associated with better outcomes. How do you create this? You do this by starting from a place of respect. Honor the relationship. See the potential in everyone. Encourage each student to express her joy.

Judge everyone by their own yardstick. This means that you consider their own talents, goals, and abilities, and don't compare them to others.

Make sure that your class policies apply equally to everyone. If Samia doesn't get to dance in the recital because of missed practices, then Malika can't either.

Be dependable. Do what you say you are going to do when and how you say you are going to do it. If you tell a student that if she does X, Y, and Z, she can move up to the next level, you have to honor that with every student. Don't make shortcuts just because it is convenient for you. Don't hold others back because they have other deficiencies that you don't like.

Create a supportive environment by encouraging students to follow their own heart in dance and show that vision to others.

Success is also related to sincerity. I am not lavish in my praise, but when I give it, the receiver always knows that it is genuine. I am true to my personality and that doesn't change. What is genuine to me will be different from everyone else.

Be aware that confrontational feedback styles are not usually motivating. I am not denying that there are rude, confrontational teachers with full studios and talented students, but this is not the most effective way of producing growth in students. Be honest, direct, explain your feedback, and give suggestions on what could be done better in a supportive manner.

Here are some examples of appropriate use of feedback:

When you pull your shoulders together like that (demonstrate what "that" means*), you are using more effort than is required. This also pulls your body out of alignment. Relax your shoulders like this* (showing what you mean). *Can you see the difference?*

When you say, "When you pull your shoulders together," you are critiquing a specific thing. This makes it less likely that the student will take this as a personal attack and will listen to what you have to say. This also gives her something specific to work on.

When you say, "you are using more effort than is required. This also pulls your body out of alignment," this let's her know that your observation is objective and not just opinion. This makes it more likely that she will see the reasoning behind your critique and will be motivated to correct it.

Saying, "Relax your shoulders," and following that with a demonstration gives her the opportunity to see how to fix it.

Asking, "Can you see the difference?" creates an opportunity to ask questions if she is not sure what you mean.

Here is another example:

Wow! Your performance of that piece has really improved over last week. You really have mastered taking the bounce out of that spin. Your audience contact was a lot better. That combination that we have been working on still needs work on isolating the parts. Overall, it's a big improvement. I can tell you have been working hard.

This feedback uses the classic "sandwich" approach of surrounding the negative feedback with compliments. It tells what she did well, gives her specific feedback on what still needs to be done, and wraps it up with motivating statements to keep her moving in the right direction.

Be careful not to say "but" when using the sandwich technique.

Example: "I liked this, but I didn't like that."

It's easy for the listener to only hear the part that came after the "but."

Be sure to pay attention to body language when you deliver feedback. Focus your attention on the person you are speaking to. Speak with a smile on your face and in your voice. Harshness and distraction can make your words land less gently than intended.

Finally, I want to say that the student will live up to the instructor's belief. If the instructor believes that the student can succeed, the student will believe it, too. If the instructor believes that the student will fail, she will fail or leave. So it's very important that teachers cultivate a positive attitude and learn to see the potential and actualization of each student. (For more on how to build a strong relationship to help students grow, see the book on motivational interviewing in Resources for Further Study).

If you implement all the structural suggestions from chapter one, adapt your teaching style so that all styles of learners can be reached, and expand your knowledge of the dance, your classes will be fuller and more successful. If you do not have a safe, supportive atmosphere in your classroom, you are limiting your success. The bottom line is your students need to trust you. They need to trust that you know what you are doing and that you will keep them emotionally safe. It's not easy for a student to put herself on display when there is a risk of feeling ridiculed. Even if students never dance alone, it can feel as if they are on display. If you don't believe in them, they may never gain the confidence required to show you or anyone else that they can do this. So check your attitude and make sure that it is one that inspires trust and confidence.

Critiquing Yourself

When I first started out as a teacher, I didn't self-critique. If I got through the lesson without any major gaffes, I felt like I did a good job. I did critique other teachers, though. I watched them for what they did well and what they didn't do well. I learned new techniques and learned what not to do. This is good, yet the best teachers are always doing self-critique too. I don't mean that you should second guessing everything you do and wondering if you could do better. I mean that you objectively examine what happens and look for opportunities to improve.

For example, let's say a student is struggling with a movement. You have her stand directly behind you and mimic you. That doesn't result in improvement. So you use the metronome and tap out the beats. That doesn't result in improvement either. At this point, it's nearing time for the cool down, so you tell her to "work on it" and finish the class.

That scenario would leave me feeling uneasy. That's a situation in which I would think about what happened later and see if I could come up with something different to try the next week.

Here's another example. Let's say that you use a fairly direct way of addressing problems in class. You have said to everyone that if they prefer not to be singled out, they should tell you and you will only correct them in a general way or in private. Nobody has taken you up on this, but you later find out that one of your students said her feelings were hurt because she felt that you were picking on her when you corrected her. This is another situation in which it is fair to self-critique and see if there is anything that you could have done to prevent this and what you could do to fix this.

If you go through class blindly teaching your agenda and never do any self-critique, you are missing opportunities for *your* growth. You are also missing opportunities to help your students grow. Nobody has all the answers all the time. There is always something that requires some thought, research, or outside help. Leave yourself open to that. Look at what you do in class. Did you come adequately prepared? Did you communicate effectively? Did you bring outside influences into the class? Were you fair to people? Do your policies need to be updated? Is there something more you need to learn?

Maybe you are doing all you can. Self-critiquing doesn't mean you are always wrong or not doing all you can. It just means that you are taking a look at what you do and leaving open the option that something can be done better.

There are lots of teachers who start teaching before they are ready. Many may have just a beginner's level of knowledge. If this teacher never self-critiques and never grows, she will always be at the same place she was when she started. I was one of those teachers who started too soon. I got better by paying attention to what I was doing and how my students responded. If it worked, I kept doing it. If it didn't, I had to try to find a different way of doing things. When I saw something that worked well, I added that to my toolbox. When I saw a better way of doing things, I upgraded my technique. When research showed that there were healthier ways of doing things, I changed to keep up. Your longevity and effectiveness as a teacher depends on your growth. The easiest way to grow is to honestly self-critique.

How I Did It

I used a dry erase board for new moves, drilling, and writing down new choreography. I "mimicked" the sounds of the music while dancing choreography. I sang the moves to the tune of the song when teaching choreography. I used the "follow me" method for beginners with lots of repetition. I put my hands on students' bodies to guide them into moving the way that I wanted them to. In short, I used all the techniques stated here for teaching class.

Once students got to the intermediate level, I encouraged them to dance in our monthly student shows. Each student got a written critique of her performance. The expectation was that there would be improvement in the next month's performance and the same mistakes would not be repeated. Every student met that expectation.

We also had monthly video nights during which we would study a particular style of dance. Students were encouraged to give feedback on what they saw. I commented on their feedback, either to support their observations or give other perspectives. The knowledge that they gained included the ability to discern different dance styles, see that everyone doesn't agree on what is aesthetically pleasing, and gain confidence in their ability to critique others and themselves. This also helped them to see the difference between objective and subjective criticism.

I assessed every student at the end of each session to see how well they learned the material and used that feedback to help the student reach her goals and to see if my lesson plans, teaching tools, and methods needed to be revised and improved.

Resources for Further Study

Books

Kassing, G., Jay, D., *Dance Teaching Methods and Curriculum Design, 2003.* Human Kinetics. Print.

Gough, M., *Knowing Dance: A Guide for Creative Teaching, 2000.* Dance Books, LTD. Print.

Miller, W.R., Rollnick, S., *Motivational Interviewing: Preparing People for Change, 2002.* The Guilford Press. Print.

Ready, R., Burton, K., *Neuro-lingistic Programming for Dummies, 2010.* John Wiley and Sons. Print.

Porter, P., *Psycho-linguistics The Language of the Mind*, 1995. ATG Publishing. Print.

Teaching Methods Chapter Assessment

Submit a video or DVD of you teaching an entire class of at least two people for at least 30 minutes (but no more than one hour). If you are not currently teaching, you may use people who are "students" just for the purpose of the assessment. Make sure that both you and your students can be seen and heard in the video.

The recording should show:
• your use of visual, auditory, and kinesthetic techniques
• your use of a variety of teaching tools
• appropriate use of praise and constructive criticism
• if appropriate, teaching to different skill levels
• your class has a logical structure that was designed with a specific purpose
• appropriate use of classroom management skills, including time management

Address the following topics on paper about your videotaped class:

1) Are you using the class outline you developed for chapter one? If not, who is the target population of your class? What are you trying to teach? What level are the students in this class?

2) What teaching tools did you use for this class?

3) What teaching methods did you use for this class?

4) Give examples of the visual techniques you used in this class.

5) Give examples of the auditory techniques you used in this class.

6) Give examples of the kinesthetic techniques you used in this class.

7) Identify each of your students' primary learning styles and tell me how you figured that out.

8) If you gave individual feedback, walk me through the thought process of why you chose a particular technique for feedback.

9) Do you have students of different learning levels in this class? If so, what did you do to keep the class interesting for all?

Include a self-critique with ideas on what you could have done differently to improve the class. The above items can be included in the self-critique or addressed in question/answer form. Include goals and objectives for the class.

Example of a self-critique:

My class was a drum solo concepts workshop, teaching people whom I have never met before. I prepared for beginners, as my experience indicated that that is what generally shows up for workshops; however, I had many more advanced students than I anticipated. In retrospect, I should have asked the sponsor in advance for input on this and prepared a more advanced sample choreography than what I had.

I split the class in half so that the more advanced people were separated from the less advanced people. I did this so that people would not negatively compare themselves to others, so that each side could focus on their separate instructions, and so that I could more effectively teach to each group. This was effective, but when asking them to dance for each other, I should have had the advanced group dance for the advanced group, and the beginners dance for the beginners. That was what was planned, but they didn't understand my instructions. Not sure why I didn't fix that on the spot.

I used primarily auditory instruction, as I wanted the class to hear the differences in the quality of sound, but I also used visual and kinesthetic techniques. I could have provided handouts for better recall after the class.

I used a blend of students in the demonstrations to give people examples of the many varieties of things they can do in a drum solo. I think that this gave the students more confidence in feeling that they were doing it right. I think it also gave them far more ideas than I could have given them alone.

I specifically complimented the girl who said that she was afraid of improvising, because I could see her terror.

I walked through the most difficult combination using first stage of learning techniques, because I could see that it was challenging to even the advanced students. I gave individual kinesthetic instructions to the girl in the blue leotard because I could see that she was struggling with hearing a particular section in the music. I thought that if I walked her through the piece until she had it in her body, she would respond more favorably, and she did.

When I was "singing" and "vocalizing", I was using auditory techniques. The dry erase board and class notes were for visual learners and better recall after the class. When I individually instructed the girl in the blue leotard, I was using kinesthetic techniques.

Remember: I am not expecting perfection. As you can see from my self-critique example, the point is to learn from your experiences. Don't be afraid to make mistakes. Don't be afraid of feedback. The more you challenge yourself in your assessment, the greater your potential to learn.

Teaching Methods Chapter Assessment Results

Student name:_____ Date:_____

Items are scored on a 0-5 point scale. The goal is to achieve a 3, which means that you understand the material.

0- did not attempt
1- did not demonstrate a good understanding of the material
2- demonstrated some understanding of the material
3- demonstrated an understanding of the material
4- demonstrated good understanding of the material
5- demonstrated a mastery of the material

___ Correctly identified students' learning styles
___ Understood how to use visual teaching techniques and used them appropriately
___ Understood how to use auditory teaching techniques and used them appropriately
___ Understood how to use kinesthetic teaching techniques and used them appropriately
___ Used a variety of teaching methods
___ Appropriately critiqued students
___ Used appropriate tools to reach the class and teach the material
___ Can teach to various levels in the same classroom (if appropriate)
___ Has good self-awareness and is able to self-critique objectively
___ Demonstrates good classroom management skills
___ Demonstrates good time management skills

Comments:

4 BODY MECHANICS

Goal: Students will have an understanding of body mechanics and be able to use this knowledge effectively for warm ups, stretches, cool downs, and to break down movement.

Objectives:
- Students will be able to discern when students are using injurious technique.
- Students will be able to construct a safe warm up.
- Students will be able to construct a safe cool down.
- Students will know how and when to stretch and use exercises for building flexibility.
- Students will be able to break down movement.

Introduction

This is certainly the most heavily researched part of the Belly Dance Trainer Certification program. When researching material for this chapter, I found a lot and found nothing. First, I could find absolutely no research that was specific to Middle Eastern dance. Second, the research that exists on injury prevention is contradictory, so it's hard to know what is worth passing along to you.

I have taken many classes in anatomy for exercise, read tons of books, and have studied bodywork (as it relates to releasing tension and energy that keeps us mentally and physically unhealthy). I have done my best to synthesize all the information I have and make it useful to you, but I am not an expert in physiology. You are encouraged to expand your awareness of this area and keep it current as information continues to change.

In an effort to keep the program accessible to people of all backgrounds and all levels of educational attainment, I decided to refrain from using specific anatomical names so that all could understand. While I realize that this means that the information presented could be more specific, I prefer to sacrifice specificity for clarity, as this is not intended to be an anatomy class.

The information provided under all headings is not intended to be all-inclusive. There are more stretches, warm up movements, strength enhancing exercises, and dangerous moves than those that are listed here. The information in this chapter and all chapters is intended to be an overview of basic information.

Injury Prevention

Environmental Factors

Safety in dance starts with the environment, so let's start off by looking at your dance surface. Studies are conflicted with regards to whether shoes enhance safety or not. Some studies show that dancers who wear shoes have more problems than those that don't. Other studies contradict this. Some studies suggest that results vary depending upon the type of shoe and the type of activity performed. My advice is, if you are teaching class or performing in a space that has an uneven surface, protruding nails, is unclean, or is prone to have liquids or food spilled on it while you are using that space, wear dance shoes. Not just footwear, but shoes that are specifically designed to protect your feet while dancing.

Another issue to consider regarding dance surface is the slope of the floor. Raked stages are more dangerous than those that are flat. The slope of the floor makes it not easy to maintain balance, so if you have a choice about whether or not to dance on this type of surface, avoid it. If you must dance on a raked stage, create your routine in such a way that avoids quick turns and large traveling movements.

Environmental safety also includes proper lighting. My first belly dance class was held in a home studio with dim lighting. The exotic atmosphere was enhanced by a scarf draped over the light, so that the room had a crimson glow. This is fine for parties, but when you are teaching, you should be able to see everyone clearly and they should be able to see you.

Mirrors also enhance the students' and instructor's ability to see. Students are better equipped to self-correct in a studio with mirrors. The teacher's ability to see the entire classroom is expanded with the use of mirrors. Check for other types of environmental contributors to injury and make sure that your space is free from obstruction and is well lit. Environmental causes for injury are almost completely avoidable. There is no reason why an environmental injury should happen to you.

Overuse

The most common cause for non-Middle Eastern dance-related injuries is overuse. "Overuse" simply means that the dancer had not developed sufficient conditioning to execute the movement without injury. This comes from not being warmed up, not having enough muscular strength to support the movement, or not having the flexibility to do certain movements. This can also occur due to poor training or poor technique.

Since Middle Eastern dance in its purest forms does not require a great deal of flexibility or strength, I hypothesize that if Middle Eastern dancers suffer from overuse injuries, they would most likely be related to not being thoroughly warmed up and to using poor technique. However, there is a lot of variability in dance styles, so be aware that if your particular style requires high degrees of flexibility and/or strength, your class should include exercises that build the flexibility and strength required to support those types of movements.

Proper Alignment

Using proper warm-ups and cool downs are easy ways to avoid injury. The harder thing to accomplish is injury prevention by teaching sound technique. Students have such idiosyncratic ways of moving and interpreting instruction that it takes a keen eye and diligence to spot and correct poor technique. Proper alignment is key to dancing safely. It should always be considered over aesthetics.

While teachers often describe what the basic belly dance posture is, I see enough people who do not have good posture to feel that something is not being adequately conveyed. As an instructor, I thought of posture as a simple enough thing to understand and achieve, but perhaps we teachers are taking it for granted that students know what we are talking about. Maybe it's time to take an in depth look at what "basic belly dance posture" really entails.

The feet: The feet should be between hip and shoulder width apart. Allow some variance for each student's particular build. If the hips are wider than the shoulders, the correct stance may be more comfortable if the feet are closer to shoulder width. If the shoulders are wider than the hips, the body may be more balanced with the feet closer to hip width apart.

Feet should be parallel (think parallel parking). Neither should be in front of or behind the other. The heels and toes of the right foot should be equidistant from the heels and toes of the left foot (meaning that if there are twelve inches between the toes, there are also twelve inches between the heels). Both feet should be facing forward. If there is a natural turn out to the feet or the student's feet turn in, the student may feel that her feet are facing forward, because this feels comfortable. Suggest that students give a visual check and do not rely solely on how the body feels.

Weight should also be evenly distributed throughout the foot. This means that the weight should not be more on the inside or outside of the foot, nor should there be more weight on the heels than on the balls.

The knees: "Old school" teachers have a more bent knee stance, while more recent teachers take a "soft knee" stance. Neither is "wrong," but the soft knee stance will reduce the amount of tension in your thighs, give you more power, and reduce the temptation to put weight onto the knee itself. The main things to keep in mind are that your knees should not be so bent that they go past the toe. The knees should be aligned so that you could draw a straight line from the kneecap through the center of the foot. The knee is not designed to bear weight. This alignment allows the knee to transfer weight to the feet.

The hip area: The ankle bones should be in alignment with the knees. The knees should be in alignment with the hips. The tailbone should be pointing downward toward the floor. You should be able to assume this position without engaging your abdominals. If your abdominals are engaged, you are too far forward. If you feel any tension in your back, you need to relax downward a bit. This is another position that needs to be checked in a mirror. Your natural stance may feel more comfortable and "right" because it's habitual.

The chest area: The chest should be lifted and relaxed. It should be neither puffed out nor collapsed. The shoulders should also be relaxed with the shoulder blades (in back) spread apart. If you feel the shoulders being pulled up due to tension, mentally tell them to relax down without using any force to make this happen. They should assume that position naturally. If they go back so far that the shoulder blades pinch toward the spine, you are probably using your muscles to make this relaxation happen instead of your mind. If facing forward or to the side, you should be able to draw an imaginary line through your feet, knees, hips, and shoulders. Be sure that none of these points are either forward or back of the line when facing the side.

The head area: The neck should be lifted and long. The neck should not extend forward or behind an imaginary center line. The head should not be tilted to either side. It should be centered on the neck. When looking at the body from the front, make sure that the head is balanced from front to back. It's particularly important that the head is not tilted back, because this can compress the neck.

The spine: The spine should be long and relaxed. Do not use force to make this happen. Just straighten from the top without pulling up and round at the tailbone to bring the spine into its natural S shape.

Here's how you can check for proper alignment. If you were facing shoulder out and drew an imaginary line down the center of the body, it would intersect at the ears, middle of the shoulders, center of the hip, back of the kneecap, and just in front of the ankle bone. If you were facing forward and drawing two imaginary lines to check for postural misalignment, they would pass through each shoulder, hip bone, center of each knee, and to the center of each ankle.

When the body is out of balance (not centered), it causes a chain reaction of muscle tension, which reduces power, weakens muscles, and increases the likelihood of injury. If the body is tense, the range of motion is reduced. The basic belly dance posture is designed to keep the body centered, relaxed, and in the "ready" position so that your dance is easy and healthy.

Postural misalignment should be addressed immediately. If the student understands the correct alignment, but can't execute it, the problem may be due to weak muscles. The muscles surrounding the affected area may need to be strengthened. If the misalignment is due to the bone structure, strengthening exercises will not correct this.

Misalignment happens most frequently at the shoulders, hips, knees, and ankles. Most martial arts styles are aware of this and use these points to throw the opponent off balance and gain the advantage. If you keep this in mind as you are teaching and dancing, it may make it easier to keep these areas in your consciousness and continuously correct for alignment.

Alignment should be correct when standing still *and* moving, but getting it correct while standing still should help in keeping it correct while moving. Here are some common posture errors.

Mistake One

Feet are side by side. I've heard many instructors tell their students to dance with their feet together. I think this suggestion is given to prevent a vulgar look, but it does not give you good alignment. Feet should be hip width apart for most movements. Do a hip movement (ami, figure eight, or hip circle) with your feet together, and then do it with your feet hip width apart. Which one gives you more range of motion? Which one gives you better balance? Which one allows you to execute it more easily without any extraneous movement? If you are using correct technique, the answer should be the one in which your feet are hip width apart. Never sacrifice safety for aesthetic if you want to continue being healthy.

Mistake Two

Feet are "rolled out." If the dancer stands with her weight on the outside of her feet, this creates misalignment in her knees and hips. It puts undue pressure on her calves and hips and makes her work far harder to maintain balance.

Mistake Three

Feet are "rolled in." This is also incorrect and makes it hard to stay balanced. The weight in the feet should be distributed in a front (toe) to back (heel) fashion, not side to side. It should be evenly distributed. I've heard people say that this is variable, depending on how much you are carrying in your chest or gluteus, but I disagree. When your weight goes forward or behind center, you start to engage your gluteus to help maintain alignment and balance. If your weight is centered, balance should be achieved by stacking bone on bone, not by using muscle to hold you in place. The goal is to move as effortlessly as possible. If you are using muscles just to stay balanced, you are already starting at a deficit once you start to move.

Mistake Four

Toes are lifted off the floor. I am not sure why some dancers do this, but when you have all toes in contact with the floor you increase the area that supports the body. This increases stabilization. It's up to you to know good technique when you see it and not adopt something just because another teacher or dancer does it. A very famous dancer executes some movements with her toes off the floor. This is idiosyncratic to her. Lifting the toes off the floor is not required to do any movement.

Mistake Five

Knees are facing inward. This can be caused by rolling the feet in. It can usually be corrected by simply calling attention to it. If needed, the dancer may use strengthening exercises to improve this problem.

Mistake Six

Pelvis is pushed back (duck butt). "Duck butt posture" is very common, as our print and runway advertisements seem to love the duck butt posture. It is considered "attractive", so many females adopt this without even being aware of it. This posture can push your belly and buttocks out, round the shoulders and bring the head forward—all of which result in misalignment. The lower back should rarely be rounded.

Mistake Seven

Pelvis is pushed forward. I am not sure why women stand and walk with their pelvises forward (Paris Hilton is a good example of this), but I've seen this fairly frequently as well. Both postures lead to painful movement and should be corrected. Demonstrating a hip movement using poor posture contrasted with correct posture should help the student see which one is more efficient and correct.

Mistake Eight

Chest is arched. This is another one of those super model postures. It's also an aesthetic used in other dance forms, but it is not used in Middle Eastern dance. The chest should be lifted off the diaphragm, but not tilted up. The bottom of the rib cage should remain level. The reason some students adopt this incorrect posture comes from our terminology. I was taught that the chest should be "lifted." Many visualize this by pulling up and out, when it's really only lifted up through the center of the body.

Mistake Nine

Chest is collapsed. It may be that the lifted chest image came to compensate for the collapsed chest. This is fairly easy to correct. Just have the student breathe in both postures and ask which one is more efficient. Avoid the instruction to bring their shoulder "down and back." This can compound the problem, and moving the shoulders does not usually result in a correction of the chest.

Mistake Ten

Shoulders are pulled back. This problem is fairly prevalent too. It's not a Middle Eastern posture. It results in too much tension in the upper body. The shoulders do not have to be "pinched" back to give you a confident, lifted look. If your arms are in second position (extended outward from the body) and your elbows are behind the shoulders, your shoulders are pulled too far back. If you keep the arms in front of the body, your shoulders will never pinch.

Mistake Eleven

Shoulders are too high or not level. This comes from too much tension in the shoulders. The neck, jaw, and shoulders hold a lot of tension and tend to tense when under pressure or when doing something new. If the student learns a new movement with this tension, she can unconsciously adopt the tension as part of the movement repertoire. So watch for this when training in new technique and keep breathing a part of your routine. Bringing relaxation and awareness to this part of the body is usually enough to bring the shoulders down and level them out.

Mistake Twelve

Knees are bent in basic stance. Old school instructors taught dancers to bend their knees. Stand with your body in basic stance and bend your knees. Where is your weight? It's over your thighs and feet, isn't it? Now stand so that your knees are soft. (If you don't know what I mean by "soft", lock your knees, and then relax them without bending them. That's "soft.") Now where is your weight? It's over your feet, isn't it? Which feels more balanced? Which posture feels as if you could move to it and from it with the least amount of effort? Unless you are in the habit of dancing with bent knees, it should be the one with soft knees. This is what you are always looking for in the knees—softness. Softness gives you the ability to move the hips without bouncing. It keeps the knees from reaching too far over the feet. (Knees should never go past the toe.) It keeps your weight balanced. Sometimes students adopt wrong postures because of the words we use, so if you are one of those teachers who say, "bend your knees" when you really mean, "soften the knees," perhaps you should change your terminology.

It's so much easier to teach proper technique than it is to correct poor technique, so do yourself and your students a favor and watch them carefully when teaching basics and new material. Correct early. Correct often using different modalities (visual, auditory, or kinesthetic) so that they are sure to remember the correct technique later. Teach them to self-correct so that they know when they are in alignment or not. Avoid overuse injuries by introducing new material at the beginning of class when students are less likely to be fatigued and lazy. If the material you are covering is intense, keep the duration short.

Four hour high intensity workshops have a high risk for injury, as do bellyrobics types of classes. Avoid teaching them if your students are not conditioned for that type of workout. If you want to teach responsibly, do not teach high intensity classes to students you do not see regularly and are not aware of their level of conditioning. If you teach high intensity, aerobic style classes, always include conditioning and move from a low or moderate level of intensity at the start of the session and gradually build in intensity over a number of weeks, when the students have had sufficient conditioning.

Another hint for an injury-free class is to breathe with your belly. This will help you to remember to disengage your abs when dancing. People want to suck in their guts to create a long lean look, but this reduces the amount of oxygen available. You also lose power in your hips, shoulders, and spine, and can pull yourself out of alignment because air is forced into your chest, which raises your center of gravity. (There are movements when you want to engage your abs to help support your back and maintain balance, but most belly dance movements do not require you to tighten them.)

Don't tighten your abdominals and gluteus to maintain balance. It weakens internal muscles, inhibits breathing, decreases flexibility, and can create low back pain. Habitual tension contributes to poor posture and pain.

So what about all this "dance from your core" stuff that comes from Pilates, you ask? To keep it simple, the six core muscles are found at the spine, waist, and abdominals. Some are at the surface and some are deep inside. Some of the muscles respond early to light weight-bearing loads. Some respond later, when the load is heavier or when misalignment occurs. That's why having a strong core is essential. However, this does not mean that you should engage your abs to "strengthen your core." Tightening your abs will not reach the muscles that are deep inside. It will only contribute to more tightness in the body and an increased likelihood of misalignment. You don't need to tighten your glutes or your abs to move effectively.

Let's test it. Lift your leg with your glutes engaged. Now lift your leg with the glutes relaxed. Which gave you a better range of motion? If you can stand without your gluteus and abs flexed, you don't need them for better balance or movement. The same is true for other movements. If you can do a hip circle (for example) without holding in your abs, you don't need to engage the abdominals. If you can do a shimmy without squeezing your gluteus, you don't need to squeeze your gluteus. Now, I understand that the movement doesn't *look* the same if muscles that are not required are used, but efficient movement is healthy movement. You will have to weigh in your mind if the aesthetic is worth compromising balance, making the movement harder to execute, and possibly setting yourself and your students up for injury.

If you dance with proper posture, you will strengthen your core. If you maintain a strong core, it will help you to stay in good posture. So Taaj's bottom line on "dancing from your core" is, maintain your posture and your core will take care of itself. If you must strengthen your core, cross train in Pilates, Tai Chi, qigong, or yoga with a competent teacher who will correct misalignment. Core training exercises are weight-bearing exercises that move through different postures to create strength and flexibility. If you are doing them incorrectly, you may weaken the muscles instead of strengthening them.

Maintaining Posture While Moving

It may seem simple to maintain posture while moving, but it isn't. When you are standing still and doing a movement in isolation, you aren't shifting weight. You aren't flowing from one movement to another. You aren't changing directions. So as an instructor, you can't forget about posture once you leave basics behind. Posture can become even more of a problem because students may attempt to compensate for their lack of understanding or ability by "cheating." Cheating can mean that they use muscles in the extremities, rather than the center of the body, to execute movement. It can mean that they throw themselves off balance. Either choice can result in injury.

To get students used to maintaining posture, you may wish to drill short combinations so that students become accustomed to moving from one thing to the next. If you simply teach choreography once they understand basics, you may have students who can be on stage quickly, but you may also create students with poor posture habits who don't have the ability to self correct. It's better to go slowly, instill good habits, and explain to students what skills they are developing, so that they can self-correct rather than just give them the whole enchilada (a choreography) and have them understand nothing. The student who has no knowledge of good posture and hasn't developed skills in a linear fashion is often the one who is prone to injury and can only dance moves in sequence. That's not dancing. That's memorization.

Warm-Up

Believe it or not, there is little scientific evidence that warming up prevents injury or enhances performance. However, most athletes, dancers, and exercise professionals believe that a warm-up is essential for the following reasons:

- it reduces the risk of overuse injuries
- it provides a gentle transition for mind and body from rest to heavy activity
- it increases oxygen to the muscles and puts the body in the "ready" position

A dance warm-up should last between five and ten minutes. The movements should include things that increase blood flow, lubricate joints, and quickly raise the body temperature one and a half to two degrees. The movements should be similar to those used in the dance so that the muscles used in the dance are reached. The movements used in warming up for dance should use the large muscles of the body first (as this increases blood flow and temperature quickly), progress from slow to fast, and progress from simple to complex. Warm-ups should also move the body in front to back and side to side motions before moving to rotating movements.

Warm-ups should also include breath work, for many reasons. Beginning students often hold their breath. Getting them in the habit of breathing with movement (out on effort, in on release) helps them avoid the tension that comes with not breathing. It also focuses the mind on the task at hand. If your mind is not focused, you cannot breathe deeply. If you breathe deeply, bringing air into the belly and bottom of your lungs, your dancing will be much more effortless and look more relaxed and lovely, too. When you incorporate breathing into the warm-up, you warm up the mind and body.

The warm-up should segue naturally into the class material. If you are conditioning for flexibility (stretching), do not do these exercises until after the body is thoroughly warmed up. Warm-up is for waking muscles up, not increasing flexibility. Stretching can cause tearing if the body is not sufficiently warmed up.

Here are some suggestions for warming up various parts of the body. Remember to maintain proper posture while doing all dance movements, including warming up. Remember that this is not an exhaustive list of movements. Feel free to add your own. Maintain proper posture and breathe through the movement. Repeat each movement three to four times. When creating a warm-up routine, remember to move from the large muscles to the small ones, and from simple movements to complex. If you do something in one direction, do it in the other as well.

Neck - Start in basic stance with the head relaxed and floating freely above the body. Look to the right. Look to the left. Turn the head back to center and drop the head down as if you were touching your right ear to your shoulder. Touch the left ear to the shoulder.

Shoulders - Lift shoulders either together or one after the other and release back to neutral. Repeat three to four times. Follow with relaxed, controlled shoulder rolls (remember to move in a front to back or side to side motion before rotating). Reverse direction.

Wrists - Put hands in prayer pose. Gently push the fingers so that they go first to one side, and then to the other. Follow with wrist circles in both directions.

Fingers - With hands in prayer pose and fingers facing up, gently press on each finger and release.

Chest - Gently slide the chest side to side without coming off center or involving the hips. Follow with chest or rib circles. Without coming off your center, bring the chest forward, then to the side, back to neutral, then to the other side. Reverse the direction.

Hips - Gently slide the hips side to side without coming off your center. Stop an inch or two from your full range of motion. Reverse direction. Another hip warm up is to do gentle up and down (or down and up) shimmies. You can move from slow to fast to raise the body temperature.

Thighs - Walking in a circle is another great way to warm up the legs. If you incorporate swinging arms, it will help to raise the body temperature as well. If you don't have enough room to walk, you can swing your legs in place. Simply support yourself by placing one hand on a wall, and then swing one leg back and forth in a controlled fashion. Change legs and repeat. Legs contain large muscles. Using large muscles elevates the temperature more quickly, so you may wish to start your warm-up with the legs.

Knees - While standing in place, pick your foot off the floor and swing your leg back and forth in a controlled fashion while bending at the knee. This is similar to the activity described for the hips, but a different joint is activated here.

Feet - Flex the ankle up toward the foot, then release and point the toe in the opposite direction. Follow by rotating the foot in a circular motion. Reverse direction. While standing in place, lift the toes off the ground and place them each back on the floor one by one, starting with the outer toe. The feet are most often neglected in warm-ups and cools-downs, and are often prone to injury, so be sure to pay attention to the feet.

Cool-Down

Just as you should not abruptly jump into dancing, you shouldn't abruptly stop either. Your class should always finish with a cool-down. Doing a proper cool-down gives the mind and body a chance to gradually transition from more intense to less intense activity. The cool-down also reduces muscle and joint soreness after exercise and promotes faster removal of metabolic waste.

The cool-down should last a minimum of five minutes. It should include less intense versions of movements used in class. Mild stretches that focus on the muscles used in class may also be used. Some authorities say that stretching during the cool-down is a good idea. Others say you should wait at least an hour after your work out to stretch to give muscles a chance to recover. Don't forget that rest is an important part of training and conditioning.

Using imagery during the cool-down is a good way to reinforce learning and cement any new concepts, feelings of accomplishment, and good habits into the body. You may wish to instruct your students to visualize specific positive images during the cool-down. You may simply instruct them to breathe into the movement, bring relaxation into their bodies, and create their own images of what is important to them.

Stretching

Many things inhibit range of motion, such as: muscle tightness, the presence of scar tissue, and nervousness. In order to get a greater degree of movement, you have to know the reason for the restriction of movement. When movement is restricted by muscle tightness that is not due to nervousness, range of motion can be increased through the use of stretching.

In order for stretches to be effective for increasing range of motion in dancing, the stretch needs to be done while the muscle is warm, executed for 30 to 60 seconds, and applied with low force. Stretches that are done while cold, for short periods of time, while bouncing, or are too vigorous, can cause tears in the muscle and do not result in any permanent elasticity of the muscle.

Your stretching routine should be done regularly and methodically. Some experts say that it should be done five to ten minute into the warm-up. Some say it's better to do as part of the cool-down. One thing the experts agree on is that stretching should be done with warm muscles. Use stretches that specifically target the muscles used in dance. Use deep breathing to facilitate the relaxation process.

Tips on stretching:

Never force or hold the body into a position that is uncomfortable. Stretches should be to the point of mild tension, not pain.

Stretches should be held for thirty to sixty seconds.

Maintain proper posture while stretching.

Breathe through the movement.

If your body starts to quiver, shake, or vibrate during a stretch, relax and let go a little.

Don't compare your level of flexibility to others. Everyone is different.

If something hurts, stop.

If you do something on one side, do it on the other as well.

Here are some sample stretches that you may wish to use:

Face - This may sound a little weird, but beginning students often hold tension in their faces. To relax this, raise your eyebrows, open your mouth, and stick out your tongue. Relax and repeat.

Neck - Same movement as used for the warm-up, but hold the movement for a longer period of time.

Shoulders - Same shrugs and circles used in the warm-up.

Stand with your feet wider than shoulder width. Bend the knees, but don't let your knee go past your toes. Bend forward and put your hands on your thighs. Slowly press one shoulder forward. Repeat on the other side.

Sit on the floor with your feet underneath you. Slowly relax forward with your arms outstretched in front of you (child's pose). This will stretch your shoulders and arms. It will also release tension in your lower back.

Arms - Raise your hands over your head, and then relax them down behind your head. Grab one elbow with your hand and allow the other hand to hang down behind your head. Gently pull on the elbow. (This targets the back of the upper arm, or tricep).

Start on your hands and knees with your hips and hands in a straight line with your shoulders. Turn your hands so that your fingers are facing away from your body. Keep your palms flat and lean back. This stretch targets your wrists and lower arms.

Hands - Do the same exercises listed in warm ups.

Spread fingers apart as far as they will go and hold. Bend fingers at the joints and hold. Repeat.

Reach your arms out in front of you. Lift hands so that your fingers are reaching toward the sky. Hold. Drop wrists so that fingers are pointed to the ground. Repeat.

Back - Start on your hands and knees with hands and knees shoulder width apart. Pull up through the spine while allowing your head to relax forward. Inhale and contract your stomach muscles as the spine pulls up. Exhale and return to the starting position. Be careful not to let your abdominals sag.

Abdominals - Lie on the floor facing down with your hands near your shoulders and touching the floor. Lift your chest off the floor and arch your upper back. Your hips and lower back should remain relaxed. Return to your starting position.

Legs - Stand with your feet shoulder width apart. Bend one leg and allow your weight to rest on that leg while extending the other in front of you. Flex the foot of the extended (non-weighted) leg, so that the toes are pulling in towards you. Rest both hands on your thighs for support, but do not push on the extended leg or hyperextend that leg. Keep your weight centered. Engage the abdominals to relieve any back strain. You should feel this stretch in the back of the upper leg (hamstrings).

Lie on your back with both knees bent. Clasp your hands under the knee and slowly bring the knee to the chest. Pull the thigh to your chest and hold. This stretch targets the back of the upper leg (hamstrings) and butt (gluteus maximus).

To stretch the front of the upper leg (quadriceps), stand with feet shoulder width apart. Raise one leg behind you and hold the foot in the hand on the same side of the body. (For example, if you raise your right foot, hold it in your right hand). Reach the opposite hand toward the ceiling.

Sit with one leg bent and the other straight out in front of you. Put your hands behind you for stability and lean back into your hands. Take care that the foot that is behind you is facing behind you, not out to the side. Do not let the leg come off the floor. If it does, ease up. This signals that you are over doing it. This stretch targets the front of the leg (quadricep). You can also do this with both feet underneath you.

To stretch the back of the lower leg (calf), stand with your feet together. Step forward on one leg, so that your feet are now about two feet apart. Both feet should be facing forward and in full contact with the ground. Rest your hands on the front leg. You should feel this stretch in the extended leg behind you.

Stand on a step, so that your heels are hanging off the back. Lift up so that you are on the ball of your feet. Slowly drop down so that you are below stair level. This will stretch the back of your lower legs (calves).

Feet - For an ankle stretch, use the same two exercises described in the warm-up.

Start by kneeling. Lower the body so that your weight rests on your toes. Keep your toes in contact with the ground. (In other words, don't rest your weight on the tops of your feet). Rest your hands in front of you. This stretch targets the bottom of your foot and your toes.

Start by standing and lowering yourself into a squat position. Your feet should be flat. Your hands should be inside of your knees and knees are outside of your shoulders. The knees should be in alignment with your toes (as always). This stretch is really good for those people who can do it, as it targets the knees, back, Achilles tendon, ankles, and groin. It is definitely not for everyone though, as people with bad ankles, tight Achilles tendons, and/or poor balance should not let their hips drop below their knees when doing a squat.

Strengthening

Proper strength is important because strong muscles support the dancer's movement, allows her to execute movements without cheating, and makes her body less prone to injury. For example, strong ankles support work on the ball of the foot. Strong abdominals support movement in the back.

It is important to identify weak areas and strengthen them. If you have a strong back and weak abdominals, you will generally compensate by using poor posture, bad technique, or using another body part to execute the movement. Weak muscles contribute to a lack of agility, so you may not be able to move as quickly or as fluidly as you would like. When you strengthen the body so that all parts required to move effortlessly are strong, you will have less injury, better execution, and a longer career.

Activities that promote coordination or endurance are not necessarily going to increase muscular strength. Increased strength comes from repeatedly contracting the targeted muscle. The muscle should move throughout its entire range of motion. There should be resistance, and the speed of the movement may vary. Be sure to watch the angle of the joint, as a slight change can alter what is being worked and strengthened.

Don't be fooled into thinking that you need to train with weights. Resistance is needed to build strength, but if you have too much resistance, you will create bulk. It's more efficient for dancers to use a Flex-a-ball or Swiss ball, or resistance bands for strength training. There are some great training videos using both of these products.

Here are some tips on strength training:

Whether using your own body weight, free weights, or resistance bands, control the movement. Don't use momentum to make the movement happen.

Maintain proper posture.

Breathe through the exercise. Never hold your breath.

Strength gains are achieved through a high level of resistance and low repetitions. As your strength increases, your resistance should also increase.

How Does Movement Happen?

"How are you making that movement? Where is it coming from?" Those are legitimate questions. They are questions that you should be able to answer if you are teaching.

Think about it. What if you asked me how to do a vertical figure eight and I told you to create the movement from your hips? Bring one hip up, out, down, and in, and then bring the other up, out, down, and in. What if I told you to create that movement using your legs? Your legs drive the movement, so you start in basic stance, straighten one leg while pushing the hips out to the side, and then bend the leg while bringing the hip underneath your hip bones. Then do the same thing on the other side.

Do you get a vertical figure eight using both techniques? You do. But are they the same? No, not visually and not muscularly. So which is correct? Technically, as long as the movement is not injurious, it is correct. Sometimes you want a different look that is created by varying the way the movement is done. For example, an Egyptian hip circle is not the same as a Turkish hip circle, but both are correct. However, if you want to keep your students healthy and injury free, opt for the technique that uses the least amount of effort, maintains balance most easily, and uses the muscles of your center, rather than extremities.

I once overheard Dancer A complain that Dancer B could not do leg driven hip lifts. She could only do them by driving the movement with her hips. Dancer B's technique was actually correct. Why? Which is closer to the center? Which requires the least amount of effort?

Not sure? The further the moving body part is from the center of the body, the more effort that is required to do the movement. The more body parts that are engaged in creating the movement, the more effort it takes to do that movement. That means that it is always going to take more effort to do a leg driven movement than a hip driven one. In fact, it might just be a good general rule of thumb to not initiate movement from the legs, unless it's a traveling step that takes you from place to place, of course.

Let's look at snake arms as an example of where movement comes from in the upper body. So what's moving? The arms, right? But is the movement coming from the arms? Well, let's see. The big muscles in the upper arm are the biceps and triceps. These muscles contract and release, moving the arm in an up and down pattern. That's not going to move your arms in a circular snake arm pattern. The muscles of the lower arm deal with the wrists, so that's not going to create the snake arm movement pattern either. So we should move our attention toward the body. Would the shoulders make this movement happen? Can shoulders move in a rotating pattern? Yes. And isn't that the place that usually starts hurting once we do snake arms for a while? (ding ding ding ding!) Ah! That's how you figure out where the movement originates.

Could you use arms to make snake arms? Of course, but that's not the primary mode of movement, nor could you get any rotation action without engaging the shoulders. I ask students to focus on the movement flowing from the shoulders, elbow, wrist, and fingers, but that's not where the movement is coming from. You could create variations that use more or less of the elbow, wrist, and fingers, but the movement will always come from the shoulder. If you give instructions that include where the movement comes from, it will usually result in less misinterpretation and less misalignment.

So how would you break that down? Well, we know that the movement is coming from the shoulder, so let's start there. The shoulder moves in a circular pattern from front to back. If we break that down into four steps (I like four steps), we would move the shoulder from 1) neutral, 2) forward, 3) up, 4) back (which is behind center), and back to neutral. You could slowly speed that up until the student is doing it with no pauses in a circle. From there, you can instruct the student to allow the arm to relax and follow through. Then let the energy and the ripple follow down to the elbow. Then the wrist. Then all the way out the finger tips, maintaining the circular ripple all the way down.

That breakdown takes into account where the movement happens. It breaks it down into simple, achievable steps. It moves from simple to complex. You may wish to also add directions that use auditory and kinesthetic cues.

Let's look at another example. Let's break down a combination. Assume that the student can do the move in isolation (or why else would we be doing combinations?) So the combination is a horizontal figure eight, followed by a hip circle. We will use an eight count so that each movement can utilize four counts. So the break down is: right hip front (1), back (2), left hip front (3), back (4), and around (5), and complete the circle (6, 7, 8). This is a fairly simple combination, so assuming the student knows the movement and can see and hear you, it should be uncomplicated to get them to figure this one out.

Let's break down a layered movement. We will layer hip shimmy with a hip circle. For this one we can use a four count. Start with a small hip circle (small usually = more control). Move the hips to the right of the body (1), front (2), left of the body (3), and center (4). Do that in a controlled manner before adding the shimmy. Expect that the student's shimmy will stop at some point during the rotation, but keep going. As long as they can see that YOU can do it, they will be encouraged that they will soon be able to do it, too. While I am on that topic, always adopt an attitude that the movement you are executing is doable. As long as you act like it is attainable, your students will rise to the occasion. If you act like they will never get it, they will live up to that too.

Break down just means that you know where the movement is coming from. You put it into bite-sized pieces and deliver the information in a method that they can understand. Most teachers are good at giving bite sized pieces. The place where I see them falling short is not knowing where movement comes from and not having a diverse method for delivering information.

Knowing where movement comes from just involves thinking about it, moving your own body, and looking for what takes the least amount of effort. First look at what is moving. Move from the extremities to the core and see where the energy begins. Then ask yourself what direction the moving part is moving in. Some muscles move front to back. Some rotate. Some increase or decrease the joint angle. Finally, check yourself to see if there is some other body part that would make the movement easier. If you pay attention, it will become easy.

Learn how to communicate in visual, kinesthetic, and auditory terms. Be creative. Use of simile and metaphor is great. If you say that the movement feels like chocolate, the student gets the idea that it's smooth. If you say that it feels like a freight train approaching, that translates as a quivering or vibrating movement. The right example can work for visual, auditory, or kinesthetic people because a visual person might picture chocolate, while a kinesthetic person feels the smoothness in her mouth. The visual person might see the train, while the auditory person hears it, and the kinesthetic person feels the rumbling. Either way, they may all translate that into the quality that you are looking for.

Moves to Watch Out For

There are some moves that are dangerous to do or at least require some caution when executing. Be aware of what these are and teach and execute with care.

Turkish Drop – The highest-rated move for potential danger is the Turkish drop. It requires that you spin and drop while falling backward, without being able to see exactly where you are going to land. It requires you to suddenly bend your knees and shift your weight. This movement can result in injury to the back, head, and knees.

Zar head roll/ Khaleegy hair toss - There are some really impressive pictures taken of dancers doing these similar moves. They are dramatic and impressive, but whenever you move your head that quickly and violently, you are asking for trouble. Just ask a chiropractor. (Can you say, "whiplash"?) As someone who has suffered from neck injury, I highly recommend avoiding both of these movements. These movements can also result in bruising of the brain (sort of like self-inflicted Shaken Baby Syndrome).

Floor work - Floor work is lovely, but unless you are conditioned to do it properly and have the required strength, it can result in injury. It's very strenuous and not for the casual dancer. There is rarely space or time for the proper warm-up prior to a performance, so even if you have the conditioning, it's risky.

Veil work - Believe it or not, veil work is also risky! It's done so often that people don't think of it as "dangerous", but this can result in shoulder injury.

Windmills - This movement involves stretching side to side and touching your toes with the opposite hand. This isn't a belly dance movement, but may be used in warm-ups or cool-downs. Avoid it!

Anything that uses a bounce - This was popular on all the aerobics shows in the 80s and has been shown to be injurious. There are big name instructors who have not kept up with exercise research. If you are in a workshop where you are told to do this or any other injurious technique, do not follow the leader. You are responsible for taking care of your own health.

Head movements that involve the chin touching the body and then moving the head up so that you see the ceiling - This is actually an exercise that my chiropractor gave me when I was in rehab after a car accident. It's not unsafe. The problem is that it is generally executed incorrectly. When looking up, the head should never release all the way to the back. Most people want to get the full stretch, so they extend all the way down in front and all the way up, which is dangerous.

Rolling the head in a circle - It's just a slow zar head circle. It's not recommended, as it can put stress on the cervical spine.

Deep lunges - Remember that the knee should not go past the toe. This puts weight on the knees. Knees were not designed to be weight-bearing joints.

Berber walk - Don't let the knee go past the toe. Environmental hazards, like nails on the stage, may also make this hazardous.

Grand plies/deep squats - The knee should not go past the toe. There is a tendency for non-ballet dancers to also stick the butt out and/or bend at the waist, which is potentially dangerous.

Standing straight leg toe touch - This exercise is sometimes seen in warm-ups and cool-downs. A variation is to bring the head all the way to the knees. This can be done more safely in a seated position on the floor.

There are many more movements that I could have put here. What makes them risky is improper execution or execution by a dancer who does not have the conditioning or flexibility to do them. The vast majority of dancers are hobbyists. Most classes are for hobbyists. This means that students may only dance once a week. This may mean that students do not devote a lot of time to strength or flexibility training. This can mean that a lot of students will make mistakes in their form.

Be vigilant. Know how to do movements correctly or avoid them. Give thorough explanations. Watch for errors and correct them. If you know that your class is preparing for a choreography that requires a movement that is more strenuous than usual, use class time to do some strengthening. If a new routine requires more stamina, use class time to build endurance. You are the leader. It's up to you to model proper technique and give your students the awareness that they need. Every body is different. You can't necessarily know that a particular student needs extra attention in a certain area, so make each student responsible for her own body and give her guidance so that she can accept that responsibility.

Resources for Further Study

Books

Anderson, B., *Stretching*, 2010. Shelter Publications, Inc. Print.

Andes, K., *A Woman's Book of Strength: An Empowering Guide to Total Mind/Body Fitness,* 1995. Perigee Trade. Print.

Calais-Germain, B., Lamotte, A. *Anatomy of Movement: Exercises*, 2008. Eastland Press. Print.

Clippinger, K.S., *Dance Anatomy and Kinesiology*, 2006. Human Kinestics. Print.

Cooley, B., *The Genius of Flexibility*, 2005. Touchstone. Print.

Delavier, F., *Strength Training Anatomy*, 2010. Human Kinetics. Print.

Fitt, S., *Dance Kinesiology*, 1996. Schirmer Books. Print.

Franklin, E., *Conditioning for Dance*, 2003. Human Kinetics. Print.

Friedman, L., *Alvin Ailey Dance Moves*, 2003. Stewart, Tabori & Chang. Print.

Kent Rush, A., *The Modern Book of Stretching*, 1997. Dell Publishing. Print.

Page, P., Ellenbecker, T., *Strength Band Training*, 2010. Human Kinetics. Print.

Pryor, E., Goodman Kraines, M., *Keep Moving! It's Aerobic Dance*, 2000. Mayfield Publishing. Print.

Seiger, L., *Fitness and Wellness Strategies*, 1994. McGraw- Hill. Print.

Solomon, R., Solomon, J., Cerny Minton, S., *Preventing Dance Injuries*, 2005. Human Kinetics. Print.

St. George, F., *The Stretching Handbook*, 1995. Simon & Schuster. Print.

Teleseminar CDs

"Do You Make These Common Posture Mistakes While Dancing?" featuring Shakira and Djimmah Karena- available through Taaj

Body Mechanics Chapter Assessment

Submit a video or DVD of you teaching an entire class of at least two people for at least thirty minutes (but no more than one hour). At a minimum, the class should contain a warm-up, instruction, and cool-down. Make sure that both you and the students can be seen and heard. Your video/DVD should include:

- a proper warm-up
- a cool down
- if the class uses movements that require strengthening and/or stretching, those should be shown
- instruction on proper posture
- correction for poor posture
- breakdown of technique that is appropriate to the skill level of the class

Also submit a written self-critique of what you did well and what could be improved upon.

Your video/DVD should also show:

- your class has a logical structure that was designed with a specific purpose
- appropriate use of classroom management skills, including time
- a variety of teaching techniques
- a variety of teaching tools
- appropriate use of praise and criticism
- if you have students of varying levels, you respond to this by teaching to each level

Example of a self-critique:

This class is targeted to beginners who have been studying for about a year, so they are advanced-beginners. The class used a small number of movements that the students were very familiar with, so that they could concentrate on the goal. The goal of the class was to move in and out of good posture, so that they could begin to self-correct.

The warm-up was about getting the ladies focused on transitioning from their workday into the class. It was light-hearted and fun, with easy to execute movements. I didn't do any correction during this time, because this was a warm up we use frequently, so the students were very familiar with it.

Once we got into the body of the class, I was meticulous and slow about breaking down every movement, because I wanted you to see that I could do that for beginners, but also because I wanted the students to be aware of how every transition felt in the body. I wanted them to feel when they were off center, when they were at their maximum range of motion, and if other parts of their bodies were relaxed or tensed. The mirror was very helpful, because it helped the student who was out of alignment see it. The rest of the class could also see it. When I had the class replicate the posture of the dancer who was out of alignment, they could also feel how it felt in the body.

I thought that this was a very effective class for studying alignment. Alignment is not something I have had a lot of instruction on. I didn't feel very comfortable going into this class because of that, but going through the process of creating the class and executing it with my students raised my awareness a lot! I really like this exercise and will probably do it more as we add more movement vocabulary to our repertoire.

I noticed that I used a lot more verbal instruction than is typical for me. I felt I rushed some things. I think that was because I was nervous, because the material isn't that comfortable for me yet. The students seemed to respond to what I was saying, so maybe it wasn't as bad as I thought.

This class relied heavily on visuals (seeing themselves in the mirror) and kinesthetics (observing how the movement felt in the body).

I am getting more comfortable with giving feedback without sounding apologetic. I don't wait until someone asks a question to address a problem anymore, either. This feels better for me because it seems more proactive.

I didn't feel like I missed correcting anyone. The class was so focused on alignment and things moved slowly enough that I didn't feel like anything really could be missed. I felt good about that, because it was the first time that I wasn't reviewing the class in my mind after the fact and seeing all my mistakes. Overall, it felt really good. I think that it will get better as I am more comfortable with the topic.

Body Mechanics Chapter Assessment Results

Student's Name_____ Date:_____

Items are scored on a 0-5 point scale. The goal is to achieve a 3, which means that you understand the material.

0- did not attempt
1- did not demonstrate a good understanding of the material
2- demonstrated some understanding of the material
3- demonstrated an adequate understanding of the material
4- demonstrated a good understanding of the material
5- demonstrated a mastery of the material

___ proper warm-up
___ effective cool-down
___ proper exercises that strengthen or stretch are shown (if needed)
___ instruction on proper posture
___ correction for poor posture
___ breakdown of technique that is appropriate to the skill level of the class
___ insightful self-critique

Comments:

5 MUSIC THEORY FOR DANCERS

Goal: Students will have an understanding of basic music theory and be able to use it in the classroom.

Objectives:
- Students will learn music theory vocabulary, so that they can communicate more effectively.
- Students will be able to find the "one."
- Students will be able to musically count repetitions of movement.
- Students will be able to set and maintain tempo with and without music.
- Students will be able to count on the beat and to the right time signature, or in a division of the correct time signature. (Example, if it's a 2/4, it would be acceptable to count it in 2s, 4s or 8s).
- Students will be able to use a variety of vocalizations to express the beat.

Why Do You Need Music Theory to Teach Dance?

Famed choreographer José Limón said, "Anyone who wants to be a dancer should study music. In dance, there has to be a harmony. You may know nothing formally about music, but there is still a sense of harmony; you will see that something is happening, and be with it. You have a sense of being there." I not only agree with his statement that you should study music if you are to be a dancer, but I think it's of vital importance if you plan to teach dance. Belly dance is the visual expression of music. If you don't understand the music, your capacity to be musical is greatly diminished, as is that of your students.

When I first started taking belly dance lessons, I thought that I was horrible at choreography. I couldn't get it. I developed an aversion to it because I just could not get my feet to move in the ways that I was instructed to move. Now that I have a lot more experience behind me, I realize that it was not my fault. The problem wasn't in my inability to follow directions. I did just fine putting steps in sequence when I was in marching band and drill team. The problem was that my teachers confused me. They put together music and movements that were not compatible. They did not phrase or count things in such a way that made sense. The bottom line was the choreographies were not musical.

There is an appalling lack of musical understanding in the dance world. If you are teaching someone who either has had musical training or has a highly developed sense of music, you will confound her if you go against the music or try to teach in a language that she does not understand. When I see a performer who is a bit off, or is sometimes off and sometimes on, I can guess that her primary teachers had no knowledge of music. Knowing music theory makes a difference.

Music is codified. There are lots of cute little ways to get your message across, but why not use the language that already exists? Why reinvent the wheel? If you understand music, your work will be more musical and you will be a much more effective teacher. You owe it to yourself and your students to be educated about music and the way that music and movement fit together.

Another reason why you should learn some basic music theory is that if all you have is knowledge of rhythms, you are limited to the rhythms that you know. If a variation is thrown at you, you may get stuck. If you can count, you can count anything. You aren't limited to music or rhythms that you've heard before.

If you teach in ways that are musical, your teaching methods become an example of musicality. Your student begins to understand the music without being directly taught. It's a short cut to understanding that every student should have. When you go to formally examine things like choreography, improvisation, and musicality, she will find that she already has some understanding.

Music Theory Basics

This brief course is an outline of what you need to know and a little of bit of what is nice to know. It is by no means intended to be a comprehensive course on music theory. If you've had any music education at all, this is surely review. Before I begin, you will need to learn the lingo of music, so here are some definitions.

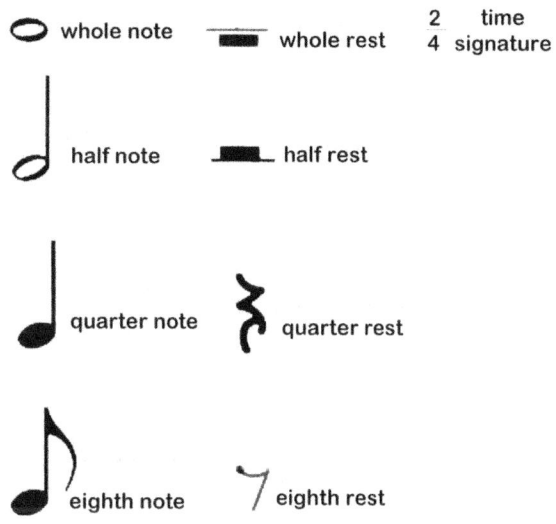

Notes

Notes are individual sounds that vibrate at a specific frequency. There are seven main notes on a western scale that go from A, B, C, D, E, F, and G before starting at A again. As you move from one note to the next note, you are moving a whole step. In western music, there are notes in between these seven notes called "half steps." (Middle Eastern music further divides the music into tones that don't exist in western music). The half step between A and B is either called an A sharp or B flat. It is the same note, but with a different name. If you raise the tone a half step, it's called a "sharp". If you lower the note by a half step, it's called a "flat".

Whole note

A whole note lasts for the entire count of a measure. For example, if your music is in 4/4 time, you know that a whole note lasts for 4 counts, because the top number of the time signature is a "4". Another way to look at this is that the note last the "whole" time. If I were playing a whole note in 4/4 time, I would count this, "One, two, three, four" and start playing it on "one" and end at the end of "four". If your time signature is ¾, the whole note only lasts for three counts.

The symbol for a whole note is an empty oval. Only one whole note can fit in a measure because it uses all the time allotted for that measure.

Half note

A half note lasts half as long as a whole note. So if you are in 4/4 time, you can fit two half notes into this measure because 2 (the value of a half note) plus 2 = 4 beats. You would count this measure 1- 2 (for the first half note) 3- 4 (for the second half note). So the first note would last for 2 counts and the second note would last for 2 counts. If these were movements, the first move or combination would take 2 counts and the second move or combination would take 2 counts.

The symbol for a half note is an empty oval with a stem pointing up or down.

Quarter note

The next smallest note is the quarter note. As you might have guessed, this note lasts a quarter of the time as a whole note, or half of the time of a half note. You could put four quarter notes into a measure in 4/4 time. Each note would last for one count. You would count this 1 (for the first quarter note), 2 (for the second quarter note), 3 (for the third quarter note), 4 (for the fourth quarter note). A quarter note looks like a filled in oval with a stem.

Eighth note

The next smallest note is an eighth note. This note lasts half the time of a quarter note. You can fit eight notes into a measure in 4/4 time. You would count this 1, and 2, and 3 and, 4 and. Each word corresponds to the time value of an eighth note. An eighth note looks like a filled in oval with a curved flag on it that can point up or down.

Sixteenth note

The next smallest note is a sixteenth note. This note last for half the time of an eighth note. You can fit sixteen sixteenth notes into a measure in 4/4 time. The most common way to count this is one-e-and-a, two-e-and-a, three-e-and-a, four-e-and-a. Each one of those words corresponds to the time value of one sixteenth note. A sixteenth note looks like a filled in oval with two flags on it that point either up or down.

There are even smaller notes, but these are all you should need for our purposes of music theory for dance.

Rest

A rest is a symbol that signifies that you are to make no sound. It's a pause in the music. The symbol for this varies, depending upon the length of the pause. There are whole rests, half rests, quarter rests, eighth rests, and so on.

When the music stops, in most cases the dancing should also stop. This can be a really important bit of information in teaching steps, combinations, and choreography. I see people dancing right through a rest all the time as if it wasn't there. I've also been in classes where someone is trying to teach a combination with a rest in it, and everyone is fouled up because it isn't given any time in the count. Pay attention to the rests! It's not empty space. It's a pause that lasts for a specified amount of time. Count it.

Scale

If you hear eight successive (meaning that each note is a full step apart) notes within an octave, you have just heard a scale. If you've ever heard anyone sing, "do, re, mi, fa, so, la, ti, do," you've heard someone singing a scale. Scales go up and scales go down. In Middle Eastern music, if you hear a scale, your movement should follow the direction of the scale. If it goes up in pitch, your body should go up or you should be dancing with the top of your body. If it goes down in pitch, movement should be traveling downward or focused on the lower part of your body. Why? Because it's musical.

Staff

Music is written on a staff. A staff is a composition of lines and spaces with various symbols placed upon it that allow you to know what notes to play, for how long, in what key, and at what tempo.

Clefs

Clefs are symbols used to show the pitch of all the notes on the staff. The treble clef indicates that the notes are in the higher registers. The treble clef is generally used to write music for instruments that produce high-pitched sounds, such as the violin, flute, and clarinet. The bass clef is generally used for instruments that produce sounds in the lower ranges, such as a string bass and tuba. Percussion instruments have their own clef called the percussion clef. This clef is used for instruments that do not produce specific pitches when played. There are other clefs, but these are the most common.

Measure

A measure is the number of beats in a phrase. This will be determined by the time signature. A measure can have many different types of notes in it, but the total value of the notes must always equal the value allotted to each measure. For example, in 4/4 time, you have four beats. That can be expressed by having one whole note, two half notes, four quarter notes, eight eighth notes, sixteen sixteenth notes, or a half note and two quarter notes, two quarter notes and four eighth notes, or any combination that gives you four counts. The end of the measure is marked by a bar.

Time Signature

The time signature tells you how many beats are in a measure and what note is used for the basic beat. The time signature is written as a fraction. The top number signifies how many beats are in the measure. The bottom number signifies the note used as the basic beat. So 4/4 time would indicate that there are four beats per measure and a quarter note is used as the basic beat. If your time signature is 9/8, you would have nine beats per measure and the eighth note would be your basic beat. In dance, the number you want to pay attention to is the top one.

Rhythm

Rhythm is defined as the pattern of regular or irregular pulses caused in music by the occurrence of strong and weak melodic and harmonic beats. Some typical rhythms used in Middle Eastern dance are: Maksoum (4/4), Ayoub (2/4), and Karsilama (9/8). As you can see, different rhythms have different time signatures.

Tempo

Tempo indicates the speed at which music is played. It is most accurately counted in beats per minute. Tempos are usually qualified by Italian terms such as grave (very slow), lento (slow), andante (walking tempo), allegro (fast), and presto (very fast). The tempo of a song does not always have to be maintained throughout the piece. The tempo can change abruptly or gradually. The tempo is either set by the composer of a written piece of music (think choreography) or by the performer (think improvisation).

Beat

The beat is the mental, audible, or visual marking of time divisions of music. The mental beat is what is felt within the body. The audible beat is what is heard with the ear. The visual beat is what is written on the musical score. A musician may describe the beat as having four counts, while a dancer may say that it has eight. Both could be correct, because anything that can be counted as four can be counted in eight. (Eight is two counts of four.)

Downbeat

The downbeat is also called the "one." It is the first beat of the measure of music. It is signified by the downward swing of the conductor's wand when an orchestra begins. It is usually the strongest pulse in the measure. If you count evenly spaced intervals between the first downbeat and the next downbeat, that will tell you how many counts there are in the measure. *This is very important if you are to count correctly.*

Double Time

Double time (or duple time) means different things to the dancer and musician. To the musician, duple time is when beats are grouped in twos, with one strong beat followed by a weak beat, which could sound like DUM, dum; DUM, dum; DUM, dum. To the dancer, double time usually means that the movement is occurring at twice the speed. (Think of the soldier marching at double time.) So if you were moving with the beat and each beat has one note per beat, you'd count that, "one, two, three, four…" and have one movement per beat. If you were moving at double time, you'd have eights beats in the same space. It would be counted, "one, and, two, and, three, and, four, and…" There would be one movement per beat, but twice as many beats/movements occurring in the same time period.

Half time

In music, half time refers to a doubling of the tempo so that each note is half as long and one measure is expanded to two. In dance, half time means that the tempo is cut in half, so you are moving half as quickly.

Triple time

Triple time means that there are three beats to the measure. Examples of this would be 3/4 time.

Triplet

A triplet is three notes of the same value that take up one beat. For example, in 2/4 time, there are two beats per measure and quarter notes are the basic beat unit. So, a measure can be made up of two quarter notes, a quarter note and two eighth notes, four eighth notes, or any combination of notes that equal two beats. One triplet using eighth notes would use three eighth notes to occupy one beat. If there were two per measure, it would be counted, "One and a, two and a" instead of "One and two and" (for four eighth notes) or "one e and a, two e and a" for sixteenth notes.

Dancers often use the terms triple and triplet interchangeably. They are not the same thing.

Determining How Many Beats Your Music Has

At the beginning of a written musical piece, you will see a number that looks like a fraction. The top number on your time signature will tell you how many beats the music has. The bottom number tells you the note value of the basic beat. Don't worry if you don't have written music. You can use your ear to tell you how many beats the music has.

Knowing the beat is important because if you can't hear the beat, you can't count it. Fortunately, most belly dance music is either in 4/4 time or in a time signature that can be divided by two. It's quite typical in dance to count anything that has an even rhythm in counts of eight.

One "cheater" way to determine the timing of your songs is to learn rhythms. Once you know the time signature of certain rhythms, you don't have to hear it or think about it. You just know. For example, Saidi and Maksoom are both 4/4. The zar rhythm, Malfoof, and Fellahi are both 2/4, but can be counted using a four count. Masmoudi is an 8/4, but can also be counted as a 4/4. I will get into rhythms in a later chapter. For now, let's look at using our ear to find the number of beats a piece of music has.

When you are trying to find the count, start with the strongest beat. That's usually going to be the "one." Begin counting at even intervals until the strongest pulse repeats. Practice first using drum music, because it's often easier to hear the rhythm in percussive pieces. As your skill builds, practice using music with different time signatures. The more you do this, the more developed your ear will become.

Be careful to give each count the same amount of time value. You aren't counting the number of *notes*. You are counting the number of *beats*. Remember that a rest also has to be counted.

There are a couple of things that may trip you up, so watch for these (although they are unusual in Middle Eastern music). Sometimes the first beat of a measure is a rest. If you start counting on the first sound, you may think that there are fewer beats per measure than there actually are. You can test this by continuing to count. If it's off on the first count, go with what is most consistent and you will find the correct number of beats.

Be careful with 3/4 time. Three four time has three beats per measure with the basic note being a quarter note. Dancers often confuse this with 4/4 time, if the fourth beat is a pause. Pauses count as beats!

The difference is this: if the beat is counted, "ONE, two, three; TWO, two, three," or "One and a, TWO and a," that's three four time. This is the same time signature that polkas are done in.

A walking three quarter shimmy is in 4/4 time. One hip moves on the first beat, the other hip moves on the second beat, the other hip moves on the third beat, then the hips stop while you change weight and step on the fourth beat. This pattern is counted, "One (move), two (move), three (move), four (pause)."

If a song starts with pick up notes as above with "Happy Birthday", this can also throw you off if you start counting beats at the first sound. Count a few measures and listen for the one. This will get you back on track.

Let's spend a little more time reviewing time signatures, beats per measure, and notes.

Let's say our time signature is written as 1/4. This means there is one beat per measure because the top number is a one. The quarter note is the basic note used in this time signature because the bottom number is a 4. If there is a quarter note in this measure, there can only be one because there is only one beat and quarter note takes up the whole measure. If the notes were 1/8 notes, there could be two because $1/8 + 1/8 = 1/4$.

Now let's say that our time signature is written as 1/8. This means that the eighth note takes up the whole measure. Both 1/4 and 1/8 are unusual, but these examples are included to show that it is possible. You could have 7, 9, or even 10 beats per measure. This example uses the eighth note as the basic beat (signified by the bottom number being an 8).

If we had 2/2 time, this would means that there are two beats per measure and the basic note used is the half note. Each note gets one count.

In our final example, let's say we have 6/8 time. There are six counts per measure and the 1/8 note is the basic note used.

All these are atypical. The time signatures you will most often encounter in belly dance music are 2/4, 4/4, and 9/8.

WARNING - BEWARE OF THE "DUMMY BEATS"!

Arab music sometimes has a strange phenomenon where the music has been flowing along in eight count phrases and then suddenly stops at four. Those four beats are what Miraj affectionately calls, "dummy beats" because they don't flow along with western musical construction, so a dummy must have created it. (Just a culturally insensitive joke.)

It's easy to be tripped up by this, so I am just putting it out there so that you are aware of it. If you are counting, everything is going along smoothly, and you suddenly trip up on a measure that is too short, it's not you. It's the dummy beats.

Using Counts in the Classroom

Knowing how to count is vital for classroom work. Working with teachers who could not count gave me the biggest learning problems. I not only had to block out what they were telling me, but I had to interpret it into meaning I could understand before I could work with their instructions. Here are some of the things that have jammed me up.

If they were a problem for me, I am sure they are problems for other students, so *don't do this*:

1) *Counting repetitions*. It's fine to count repetitions if you count them musically. For example, if a choreography requires you to repeat the same eight-count movement phrase two times, don't count "1, 2, 3, 4, 5, 6, 7, 8, 9, 10, 11, 12, 13, 14, 15, 16.." Count it *1*, 2, 3, 4, 5, 6, 7, 8; *2*, 2, 3, 4, 5, 6, 7, 8…" Dance typically uses eight counts for movement rather than the four that are used in music. If the movement that is being repeated lasts for eight counts, counting the number of eight counts in the way described above will keep you on count and also let you know how many times the phrase has been repeated. Additionally, it is more consistent to say that this phrase lasts for two counts of eight, rather than sixteen counts.

2) *Not using "…5, 6, 7, 8" to set tempo*. I think that some people use this count off system because they've seen it done. They think that this is the thing to do, but they don't know how or why. "…5, 6, 7, 8" is there to set tempo. Whatever you do after that is supposed to occur at the same tempo that you just spoke the words, "…5, 6, 7, 8." So don't say, "…5, 6, 7, 8" slowly and then start to dance quickly. Each beat corresponds to a set amount of time, so make sure that each count represents the same amount of time. If you need practice with this, follow along with a metronome.

3) *Use steady counts that stay on the beat*. The count should not speed up and slow down depending upon the speed of the music. You don't count, "1……..2,3,4, …5…, 6………, 7,8." You're not just counting to get to eight. The point is to follow the beat for eight counts and keep it consistent. Maybe the correct count for the above is something like, "One, two, e and a, three, and four, five, six, seven, and, eight." This last example shows how the number of notes can change without changing the tempo.

When you relate music to movement in the classroom, you are essentially modeling how to count, how to listen, how to portray someone else's interpretation of the music, and hopefully develop the student's ability to interpret it for herself. If you are not working *with* the music, you are not making it easier for your student to learn. Work with the music. When the sound, movement, and visual elements work together, everything flow harmoniously.

Here are a couple of examples of how to count using written notation:

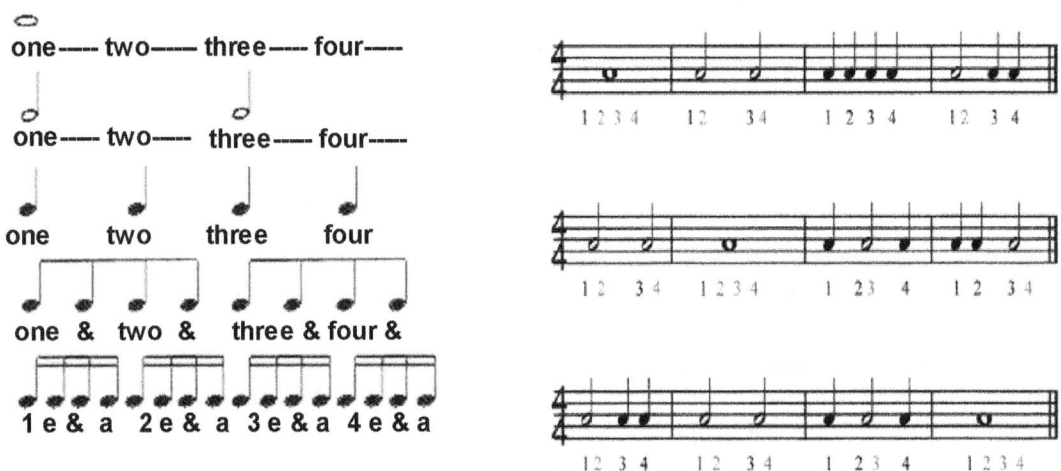

Here are some things to remember for review:

When counting, it is most correct to only count to the number on the top of the time signature, as that is how many beats there are in the measure. It is acceptable to use four counts or eight counts in dance, however, if the music does not have an odd time signature.

The value of the notes in each measure should equal the time signature (there are a few exceptions, such as when pick up notes are used). So if we were looking at the music above, we would know that the value of the notes in each measure should equal 4/4. In the first measure, we have two half notes. 2/4 + 2/4 = 4/4. The second measure has one whole note. 4/4 = 4/4. The third measure has a quarter note, a half note, and another quarter note. 1/4 + 2/4 + 1/4= 4/4. The final measure has two quarter notes and a whole note. 1/4 + 1/4 + 2/4 = 4/4.

Be careful to give the notes the appropriate value of time. An eighth note gets one full beat in 6/8 time, but only half that in 4/4 time.

If you have odd time signatures, it is often easier to chop up the beats. For 6/8, you may wish to count it as "ONE, two, three, FOUR, five, six," or "one, two, three; one, two, three." If you prefer to use words for this, you could say, "one, lah, lee; two, lah, lee."

A 7/4 can be counted "one, two, three, four; one, two three" or "one, two, three; one, two, three, four" or "one, two; one, two, three; one, two," as well as "one, two, three, four, five, six, seven."

For a 9/8, you can count it "one, two three; two two three; three two three," or "one, two, three, four; one, two, three, four, five," as well as "one, two, three, four, five, six, seven, eight, nine."

Chopping up the beats into evenly spaced counts will work for any odd time signature, but be aware that not all 9/8s (for example) are the same. Music from different areas will have different nuances and will be accented differently. So while the count will be the same, the accent or pulse may change. Figuring these nuances out is a good way to identify where music is from. For example, a Persian 6/8 is accented completely differently from a Moroccan 6/8, even though they share the same time signature.

If all of this is just way too confusing, you can "cheat" by thinking of everything in terms of twos or threes. Four and eight counts can be divided into twos. Sixes and nines can be divided into threes. So, if you can find the one, start counting there and notice if the count starts over at two or three. If it starts over at two, you know it's either a 2/4, 4/4, or 8/4 time signature that can be counted in twos, fours, or eights. If it starts over at three, you know it's either a 3/4 (rare in Middle Eastern dance), 6/8, or 9/8. These are most easily counted as threes. While the count may not match the actual time signature, you will always remain on beat by using this system, so it's fine. The point is more to understand how to feel the pulse, rather know the correct time signature.

Putting Music with Movement

Once you start putting movement to music, the way that you count can change. It's perfectly all right to use eight counts for everything (if it's not an odd time signature), but it may be more effective to verbalize the actual length of the movement to help the student get a feel for the musicality of the piece. For example, let's say that you have a phrase that is a series of eighth notes and the choreography is to shimmy with each hip moving with each eighth note. Rather than counting, "one, two, three, four, five, six, seven, eight," it may be better to match the speed of the movement by saying, "one, and, two, and, three, and, four, and, five, and, six, and, seven, and, eight, and." If the music is the same, but the dancer is shimmying at the half the speed, then it would be better to verbalize it one count at a time, because this matches the speed of her movement at half time.

You don't always have to count to keep tempo. You can use words or sound fragments to illustrate movement. Be creative with your voice. What you vocalize can give a sense of the quality of the movement and music. For instance, you could count, "One, two, three, Two, two, three," or say, "DA ka ta, DA ka ta," or say, "LA dee dee, LA dee dee," and convey a totally different feeling. The first example keeps time, but says nothing about the quality of movement. The second is definitely more percussive in feeling while the last is more flowing and smooth.

Exercises for the Student Who Aren't Getting It

1) Have the class clap at a set pace. Instruct the class to do some sort of movement at the same pace. For example, the students can pat their feet to the tempo of the clapping. They can do a hip drop on each clap. They can do a chest lift. Once they get the hang of one tempo, change the tempo to make it either faster or slower. The goal is to keep the tempo steady. Be sure to neither speed up nor slow down. You can check this by setting the tempo with a metronome.

2) Instead of clapping, students can use a traveling step. One step equals one beat. Students can move throughout the room using various directions and sizes of movement.

3) Divide the class into two groups. Set a moderate tempo on the metronome. Have one group use traveling steps at tempo and have the other group move at either half or twice the speed.

4) Chose music with different time signatures. Have students pair up and stand in two circles. One person of the pair will stand on the inside of the circle while the other is outside the circle. The person on the outside will clap out the beat while counting (so if it's an Ayoob, she will say, "one, two, one, two…") The person on the inside of the circle will move on the beat. Partners will exchange places periodically. Once everyone has had a chance to be in the middle, you can process what they saw and felt. Be sure to include different time signatures, such as 2/4, ¾, 4/4, 6/8, and 9/8.

5) Set the metronome to a moderate tempo. Have the students make two circles. Half are on the outside of the circle. The other half will stand on the inside, facing the outside. The ones on the outside will clap on every beat. The dancers on the inside will clap in double time so that they are clapping twice per beat. The outside group moves to every beat. The inside group moves twice as fast. Each person takes turns being inside and outside the circle. When everyone has had a chance to be in both places, process what was seen and felt. Once you have completed that exercise, change it so that the inside group is moving on the beat and the outside group is moving at twice the speed.

6) Set the metronome to a moderate tempo. Have students make a big circle. Students should clap out the tempo of the metronome. As each student is ready, have her enter the circle and dance either to the beat, at half the speed of the beat, at twice the speed of the beat. More than one student can be in the center at a time. The goal is to maintain whatever tempo each dancer sets for herself. Allow students to take turns maintaining tempo by clapping and maintaining tempo by dancing. Process how it looked and felt afterward.

7) Put on some music. Have some students make a big circle and clap out the tempo. Students should clap loudly on the one and softly on the other beats. The rest of the students will be in the center of the circle. The dancers in the middle can only move on the one. Take turns so that every dancer can clap out the beat and move in the middle.

8) Variation of #7. Instead of only moving on the one, dancers may move on all beats, but must accent the one. Another variation - students can only move on the "two."

9) Set the metronome to a moderate or slow pace. Pair up dancers. One pair at a time will use the space while the rest of the class watches. One person in the pair will set the tempo by traveling on the beat. The other dancer will move alongside her partner, but will experiment with the beat by sometimes moving twice as fast, sometimes half as fast, or sometimes moving at the same pace as her partner. For example, if dancer A is setting the pace by stepping on "one, two, three, four," dancer B may be stepping on "one and, two e and a, three, four and…"

10) For the last exercise, dancers will be moving to one of the following counts:

a) one, two, three, four

b) one and two and three and four and

c) one, two e and a, three, four e and a

Count off dancers so that everyone is either a one, two, or three. Set the metronome to a moderate pace. Cue the ones to start dancing to the tempo a. They should maintain the same movement pattern. This can either be established in advance or can be improvised. Once the ones are established, cue the twos to start dancing to tempo b. Once they are established, cue the threes to start dancing to tempo c. Make sure all groups start on the one.

Hints for If You Get in Trouble

If you are the type of person who has trouble setting the tempo, staying on beat, hearing the beat, or moving at a steady pace (and there are a lot of you, so don't be embarrassed), stop when you lose the beat. Regroup and start again on the one. There is nothing more frustrating than following someone who isn't on beat. If you lose the tempo consistently, drill with a metronome. Often simplifying the auditory stimulation will help you stay on beat because there are fewer sounds to concentrate on compared to dancing with music. Once you get the hang of working with a metronome, use only drum solo music, then work your way up to songs with several instruments.

Sometimes when we are learning something new, we start to mess up because we have to focus on putting things together. (Remember how students learn in chapter two)? If you start getting off beat when teaching something new, simplify. Slow down. Or count off to the side and let the students do the movement at tempo.

Some of the hints I've given in this chapter may help you get around the counting part. If it is easier for you to use vocalizations, use them. Just make sure to use them on beat.

If you are teaching a new rhythm to the class or a new time signature (or any other topic for that matter), make sure that you are thoroughly comfortable with the topic before trying to teach it. If you make mistakes and have to start over a lot or break it down for yourself, your students will become very frustrated. They won't likely learn much either. Students gain competency by repeating the same *correct* movements over and over again. If they cannot guess which version you gave them was correct, they won't understand or retain the information.

If music is a very sore subject with you, you might want to reconsider teaching until you have a handle on it. Understanding music is essential to conveying dance. You have to be in touch with the rhythm to teach well. Practice on your own in private. Listen to music. Rehearse finding the one. Rehearse counting. Rehearse counting at different tempos. Practice moving from double time to half time. Ask questions. Read this chapter over and over until you can clearly hear what is being conveyed and can explain the same thing to others.

The time and effort are worth it. Once you understand music, it will be like your world has gone from black and white to color. It will give you a broader means to express yourself, both on stage and in the classroom.

Resources For Further Learning

Books

Kaplan, R., *Rhythmic Training for Dancers*, 2002. Human Kinetics. Print.

Miller, M., *The Complete Idiot's Guide to Music Theory*, 2005. Alpha. Print.

Pilhofer, M. Day, H., *Music Theory for Dummies*, 2011. For Dummies Print.

Teck, K., *Ear Training for the Body: A Dancer's Guide to Music*, 1994. Princeton Book Company. Print.

Music Theory Chapter Assessment

Submit a video or DVD of you teaching an entire class of at least two people for at least thirty minutes (but no more than one hour). This should not be a class on music theory, but a class that demonstrates your understanding of music theory. You can use improvisation, choreography, drills, exercises, or whatever can best illustrate that you understand music theory. More than one rhythm and time signature should be used in your class. Make sure that both you and the students can be seen and heard. The video/DVD should show:

- you understand where the "one" is (so your count should start on beat)
- you understand how to count repetitions (so your combinations or choreography should show repetitions of the same movement phrase)
- you can set the tempo with and without music (so you should count off to set the tempo and count with music to the tempo)
- you can maintain the tempo with and without music
- you can effectively count when music and movement are put together
- you can change the speed of the movement while maintaining the tempo (use double time, half time, etc.)
- you can mark time with vocalizations other than counting (for example using words like "quick, quick, slow" or "dum tek a tek"

Your video/DVD should also show an understanding of all the material we have covered thus far.

Include a self-critique with ideas on what you could have done differently to improve the class.

Remember: I am not expecting perfection. Don't be afraid to stretch yourself. Attempt something that you are unsure about. Don't be afraid of feedback. The more you challenge yourself in your assessment, the greater your potential to learn.

Example of a self-critique

This class was targeted to advanced beginners (those who have been studying for about six months). The class was about exploring variations of simple movements by changing the tempo. We slowed some things down and sped other things up. We changed the time signature for some combinations.

I was really excited about preparing the class because it seemed fun on paper. It was even more so when the class executed it. There was a lot of laughter when people messed up, so it seemed to take the pressure off learning something new. The class seemed to like it a lot.

When we worked with the 9/8, I could tell that I was not as comfortable with this as with the other time signatures. I expected the class to have some trouble with this, but I think if I had been more confident, they may have been too.

There were definitely times when I could have corrected for technique (like when the lady in the cropped black top kept reverting back to her habit of lifting her heels on the mayas). I wanted the students to focus on the music and get that right, so I wasn't as strict as I could have been. I did correct for poor posture whenever I saw it, however.

I noticed the woman in the green harem pants (Lynn) having trouble with the whole idea of starting on the one. After explaining the exercise to the class and working with her individually, I thought it might be best to just let her do it, feel it. I thought she might get it by experiencing it. I should have offered to work with her after class. I meant to, but just forgot about it by the time class ended.

The exercise when the students were blindfolded turned out to be a dud. I thought it might make them less self-conscious if they couldn't see anyone and nobody could see them, but it actually seemed to make them more self-conscious. It was hard picking up the energy again after that.

I am still working on creating a smooth transition to the end of the class. I think if I have a ritual that I do every class, it would be better. I think it would mentally say to me and to them that this is the end of class and not feel so abrupt.

    I thought I did a good job with this class. It felt like it flowed better than any other assessment class. Even though I wasn't 100% comfortable, I am feeling better in front of the camera, the class, and just with myself as a teacher. I think I look and feel more in control. I liked this lesson because it makes me realize how much more I have to learn. But that's a good thing!

SHAKE YOUR BOOTY

Music Theory Chapter Assessment Results

Student name:_____ Date:_____

Items are scored on a 0-5 point scale. The goal is to achieve a 3, which means that you understand the material.

0- did not attempt
1- demonstrated a poor understanding of the material
2- had some knowledge of the material
3- demonstrated a fair understanding of the material
4- demonstrated a strong understanding of the material
5- demonstrated a mastery of the material

___ can consistently find the "one"
___ can musically count repetitions of movement
___ can set tempo without music
___ can set tempo with music
___ can maintain tempo without music
___ can maintain tempo with music
___ can count with the time signature or in divisions of the correct time signature
___ used a variety of vocalizations to express the beat

Comments:

6 MIDDLE EASTERN RHYTHMS

Goal: Students will have an understanding of basic Middle Eastern rhythms.

Objectives:
- Students will be able to identify the Middle Eastern rhythms mentioned in this chapter by ear.
- Students will be able to "sing" the rhythms (using dum, tek, and ka).

Introduction to Middle Eastern Rhythms

Why study rhythms?

When I first started dancing, I wanted to know everything about everything. Most teachers could identify rhythms, so I wanted to know how to do that too. As my experience with the dance increased, I learned that understanding rhythms is not really necessary at all to become a good dancer, if you have a decent ear. I seldom encountered a Middle Eastern musician who was formally taught, so it meant nothing to him if I requested a Masmoudi followed by a Chifti-telli. He preferred song titles or tempos. I had a good enough musical ear that I didn't need to slowly break down each rhythm in order to feel it in and interpret it through my body. HOWEVER, if you want to teach, knowing rhythms will be an invaluable tool in helping your students enhance their understanding of the music, communicate with others, and to help students connect rhythms to cultures.

All students are not the same. There will be many students who need to have rhythms broken down again and again in different ways so that they can hear the differences and similarities from one piece of music to another. Not all students have a well developed sense of rhythm. Not all students learn well auditorily. So working with rhythms could be very challenging to them. If you learn how to present auditory material in ways that are seen, heard, and felt, this will increase your students' ability to improvise and interpret music tremendously.

Another reason to study rhythms is that it can help students transfer concepts from one piece of music to another. For example, if your students can identify the Saidi rhythm and know the characteristic movements and feelings that go with it, they will be able to put those movements and feelings in songs that are built entirely around the Saidi rhythm, as well as pieces that have a small break with that rhythm playing for only a few measures.

One of my pet peeves is when a student takes a stylistic move from one culture or region and applies to it another that it does not belong to without knowing why. For example, I've seen dancers take the hair tossing from Khaleegy songs and just put it in a pop song when there has been no rhythmic change or no reason why that move would logically go there. It doesn't necessarily make it "wrong", but to someone with a trained eye, it looks like the dancer doesn't know what she's doing. When you know which rhythms go with which styles of dance, you and your students will not make random choices. When you choose to go outside the established folkloric repertoire, it will be with intention and not out of ignorance. This will mean you have a greater chance of breaking the rules effectively.

Chapter five will look at the most common rhythms used in belly dance. I use the term "belly dance" here, rather than "Middle Eastern dance" because I am including areas that are not in the Middle East and are not Arab. The rhythms we will look at are: Ayoob, Karachi, Malfoof, Khaleegy, Maksoom, Saidi, Beledi, Zeffa, six-eight, Masmoodi Kabir, Chifti-telli, Karsilama, and Samai.

If you've studied rhythms before, know that the information here may not be exactly what you have learned. There are many variations of each rhythm and all possible variations cannot be covered. The most basic version will be highlighted here. Also realize that the spellings of rhythms may not be as you learned them. Arabic is a phonetic language and therefore cannot be translated exactly into English. There are a lot of distortions of information about rhythms, but for the sake of communication, I will use the information that is most widely accepted as common knowledge. For example, "Beledi" isn't really the name of a Middle Eastern rhythm. However, if you want to communicate with people, you have to use terminology they will understand.

There are hundreds, if not thousands, of Middle Eastern rhythms used in belly dance. The rhythms chosen for this chapter were selected based on what you will most frequently encounter, those that may trip you up, and those that can provide knowledge that can be used in a broad-based way. For example, Beledi, or some variation of it, forms the backbone of belly dance music, so that's a necessary rhythm to know. I have only danced to Karachi once in my career; however, when it was thrown in by the band at a wedding, I knew how to dance to it because I had studied it beforehand.

There are many more belly dance rhythms. I hope that learning these will make it easier for you to understand and hear others, should you wish to further your education on belly dance rhythms.

Dum, tek, and ka

Many dancers learn rhythms from drummers or dancers who learned from drummers. Therefore it is not uncommon to hear the rhythms expressed verbally in tones of dum (pronounced "doom"), tek, and ka, or something similar.

Dum is the sound that the *derbeke* (Arabic word), or *dumbek* (Turkish word), makes when you hit it in the center of the drum head. This is done with your dominant hand. The tek sound is created with the non-dominant hand. It is a high-pitched sound that comes from hitting the edge of the drum. Ka sounds like tek, but it is made on the other side of the drum with the dominant hand. This configuration allows the drummer to have greater speed. Other sounds and places to hit the drum are possible, but these are the main ones. Other hand configurations are also possible, but this is how these sounds are usually played.

The easiest way for me to discern which rhythm is playing is to listen to the number and sequence of the dums. There are many variations of rhythms, but placement of the dums rarely changes. The teks and kas will change in number. Sometimes they are eliminated. Sometimes they are added.

The basic rhythm is used here. If you understand the basic rhythm, any embellishments should not trip you up.

Two beats: Ayoob, Karachi, Malfoof, Khaleegy

Two beat rhythms are often characterized by a fast pace and a feeling of sustained or building energy. Because of this, they are often used as entrances and exits. They are often also used in the middle of songs to pick up the tempo.

Ayoob

1	e	&	a	2	e	&	a
*			*	*		*	
dum			ka	dum		tek	

Ayoob is a single dum followed by a single ka, and then another dum followed by a tek. It is used in Turkey, Egypt, the Levant (Israel, Lebanon, Syria, and the Palestinian territories), and North Africa. In Egypt, it is the rhythm used for zar, or trance dancing. In the Levant, it is used with *debke*, but is called by a different name. An example of a popular Turkish song that uses the Ayoob rhythm is "Shisheler."

Karachi

1	e	&	A	2	e	&	a
*			*	*		*	
tek			ka	tek		dum	

Karachi is a rhythm that comes from Pakistan. This rhythm is distinct because the single dum comes at the end of the phrase. Notice also that the musical notation and count is the same for Ayoob, but the sounds made on each beat are different. This makes a tremendous difference in how the rhythm sounds and feels.

Malfoof

1	e	&	a	2	e	&	a
*		*	*		*	*	*
dum		ka	tek		ka	tek	ka

Malfoof has only one strong dum at the beginning of the rhythm on the "one." This rhythm is commonly found in Egyptian and Levantine music. In the Levant, it often accompanies *debke*.

Khaleegy

1	e	&	a	2	e	&	a
*			*		*	*	*
dum			dum		ka	tek	ka

Khaleegy means "gulf." This rhythm is indigenous to the Persian Gulf area. It is sometimes called Saudi.

SHAKE YOUR BOOTY

Four beats: Maksoom, Saidi, Beledi, Zeffa

All four of these rhythms are associated with Egyptian music, but Maksoom is found throughout the Middle East.

Maksoom

1	&	2	&	3	&	4	&	a
*	*	*	*	*	*	*	*	*
dum	tek	ka	tek	**dum**	ka	tek	tek	ka

This rhythm has the dums on the one and the three.

Saidi

1	e	&	a	2	e	&	a	3	e	&	a	4	e	&	a
*		*	*	*		*		*		*	*	*			
dum		ka	tek	ka		**dum**		**dum**		tek	ka	tek			

Saidi is a folk rhythm. Saidi means "happy." This makes it a little easier to remember because the Saidi rhythm certainly has a happy feeling to it. It's associated with men's stick dancing and women's cane dancing of Upper Egypt. Some say the rhythm was created to accompany the dancing Arabian horses and the horsy type movements come from the horses. Saidi is easily identified by the three strong dums. It starts with a dum and has two strong dums in the middle. Music with this rhythm is often accompanied by the rebaba and mizmar.

Beledi

1	e	&	a	2	e	&	a	3	e	&	a	4	e	&	a
*		*		*	*	*		*		*	*	*			
dum		**dum**		tek	ka	tek		**dum**		tek	ka	tek			

Beledi is a folk rhythm. Beledi means "of the country." This rhythm has two dums at the beginning and one in the middle. Beledi sounds like Saidi, except the dums are in different places. Beledi has also been called Maksoom or Masmoodi Seghir. All of these rhythms are in the same family and are variations of each other. (Saidi and Fellahi would also be included). The difference is in the placement of the dums, the speed and the feeling in which it is played. The discussion on deciding the correct terminology will likely never end. Just be aware that different people may call different rhythms by different things. But as I said in the beginning, the variations on each rhythm are limitless. It's no wonder that different terminology is also used for what is essentially the same thing.

Zeffa

1	&	a	2	&	3	&	4	&
*	*	*	*	*	*	*	*	
dum	tek	ka	tek	tek	**dum**	tek	tek	

The Zeffa is the wedding processional rhythm that is used to welcome the Egyptian bride and groom into the reception area. Although it has lots of drums, it is not to be used as a drum solo! This rhythm has the dums on the one and three.

Six beats

1	&	2	&	3	&	4	&	5	&	6	&
*		*		*		*		*		*	
dum		ka		ka		tek		ka		ka	

There are many different six-eight rhythms used in belly dance. They are frequently used in Persia and North Africa. The dum can be in different places, depending on which six-eight rhythm it is. Here is one example that is representative of the six-eight used in the middle of "Leylet Hob."

Eight Beats: Masmoodi Kabir, Chifti-telli

These rhythms are used primarily for slow pieces.

Masmoudi

1	&	2	&	3	&	4	&	5	e	&	a	6	&	7	e	&	8	&
*		*		*		*		*	*	*	*	*	*	*	*	*	*	*
dum		dum		Tek		tek		dum	tek	ka	tek	Tek	Tek	ka	tek	ka	tek	tek

Masmoudi Kabir

1		2		3	&	4		5	e	&	a	6	&	7	e	&	a	8	&
*		*		*	*			*	*	*	*	*	*	*	*	*	*	*	*
dum		dum		dum	tek			dum	Tek	Ka	Tek	Ka	Tek	Tek	Ka	Tek	Ka	tek	tek

Masmoodi Kabir translates as "big Masmoodi." It is an Arabic rhythm. This rhythm can be identified by the dums on the one, two, and five count.

Chifti-telli

1	&	A	2	e	&	3	e	&	a	4	&	5	&	6	&	7		8
*	*	*	*		*	*	8	*	*	*	*	*		*		*		
dum	tek	ka	tek	ka	tek	tek	ka	tek	ka	tek	tek	dum		dum		tek		

Chifti-telli is used in Turkish and Greek music. Both are often intertwined with a taxim (means "improvisation" NOT "slow"). The dums in Chifti-telli are on the one, five, and six. There is a rest on count eight.

Nine beats: Karsilama

Karsilama

1	&	2	&	3	&	4	&	5	&	6	&	7	&	8	&	9
*		*	*	*		*	*	*		*	*	*		*		*
dum		tek	ka	tek		tek	ka	dum		tek	ka	tek		ka		tek

Karsilama is the most common Turkish nine beat rhythm, but is not the only one. The dums in karsilama are on the one and the five. Examples of popular songs that use the Karsilama rhythm: "Rompi Rompi" and "Mastika Mastika."

Ten beats: Samai

Samai

1	a	2	&	3	&	4	a	5	&	6	&	7	&	8	a	9	&	10	&
*	*	*	*	*	*	*	*	*	*	*		*		*	*	*	*	*	*
dum	ka	tek	ka	tek	ka	Tek	ka	tek	ka	dum		dum		Tek	ka	tek	ka	tek	ka

The Samai is used in a lot of Classical belly dance songs. The dums in Samai are on the one, six, and seven.

Audio Exercises

You may wish to obtain a copy of *Uncle Mafufo's 25 Essential Rhythms for Middle Eastern Dance* or Issam Houshan's *Bellydance Superstars: Introduction to Middle Eastern Rhythms* to help you identify the variations. Accenting the dums with the body are a great way to get the rhythm in your body. Verbalizing the dums and clapping along can help you to develop your ear.

Resources for Further Learning

Audio Recordings

Kessler, Jonathan. (1998). Doumbek Video Practice Companion. [audio CD]

Donald, Mary Ellen. (2003). The Middle Eastern Rhythms. [audio CD]

Mafufo, Armando. (2013). Uncle Mafufo's 25 Essential Rhythms for Middle Eastern Drumming. [audio CD]

Ramzy, Hossam. (1998). Rhythms of the Nile. [audio CD] Arc Music.

Workshops

Workshops by Karim Nagi

Workshops by Issam Houshan of Belly Dance Superstars

Middle Eastern Rhythms Chapter Assessment

Submit a video or DVD of you teaching an entire class of at least two people for at least thirty minutes (but no more than one hour). This class should demonstrate your understanding of the rhythms reviewed in this chapter. The class does not have to be specifically on rhythms. You can use improvisation, choreography, drills, or whatever best illustrates that you understand how to define rhythms. Make sure that both you and the students can be seen and heard. The video/DVD should include:

- Verbal breakdown of each rhythm
- Rhythm patterns and timing should be correct

Your video/DVD should also show:

- your class has a logical structure that was designed with a specific purpose
- appropriate use of classroom management skills including time
- a variety of teaching tools
- appropriate use of praise and criticism
- if you have students of varying levels, you respond to this by teaching to each level
- use of visual, auditory, and kinesthetic teaching techniques
- correction for poor posture

Include a self-critique with ideas on what you did well and what you could have done to improve the class.

Sample Self-critique:

This was a class I have taught many times, so I was very comfortable with the material. I adapted this class to show my knowledge of rhythms by just changing the music selections. Since the students weren't necessarily focused on the rhythms, this class was still appropriate for the beginner level student. I did notice that the beginner student had some trouble with the 9/8. I decided not to spend too much time on that since it was not the focus of the class and I wanted to keep the class moving. The student with the blue top is still making posture mistakes on the undulation/shimmy. I think I spent a fair amount of individual time with her, but didn't slight the other students. I thought my rapport was better during this class. I think that was because of my familiarity with this material. I didn't use the mirror as much as I could have. Since I wasn't facing forward much, this also meant that the students didn't have maximum use of the notes on the dry erase board. There was time before and after class for students to take their own notes, though. I wasn't prepared for the question about the costuming. I felt that I didn't answer it clearly enough. I will research this more and get back with her in the next class. I am becoming more comfortable with my flow of dialogue. It doesn't seem as repetitive or silent anymore. Maybe it's just my own comfort level with teaching, but it's feeling better to me. Next time I will keep class focused on only the 4/4 rhythms because it might be easier to do odd time signatures after students have a solid understanding of easier ones.

You may also wish to include comments about the flow of class, warm-up (if any), course content, or cool-down (if any).

You do not have to use this as a guideline. However, it may help you to structure your class ahead of time and organize your thoughts afterward.

Middle Eastern Rhythms Chapter Assessment Results

Student name:_____   Date:_____

Items are scored on a 0-5 point sale. The goal is to achieve a 3, which means that you understand the material.

0- did not attempt
1- did not demonstrate a good understanding of the material
2- demonstrated some understanding of the material
3- demonstrated an understanding of the material
4- demonstrated good understanding of the material
5- demonstrated a mastery of the material

___ understanding of Ayoob
___ understanding of Karachi
___ understanding of Malfoof
___ understanding of Khaleegy
___ understanding of Maksoom
___ understanding of Saidi
___ understanding of Beledi
___ understanding of Zeffa
___ understanding of 6/8
___ understanding of Masmoodi Kabir
___ understanding of Chifti-telli
___ understanding of Karsilama
___ understanding of Samai

Comments:

SHAKE YOUR BOOTY

7 FINGER CYMBALS

Goal: Students will be able to teach how to play finger cymbals using three different methods.

Objectives:
- Students will be able to explain rhythms and patterns using drum sounds.
- Students will be able to explain rhythms and patterns using numbers.
- Students will be able to explain rhythms and patterns using R/L fingering.
- Students will be able to combine numbers and drum sounds when teaching.
- Students will be able to combine numbers and R/L fingering when teaching.
- Students will be able to combine drum sounds and R/L fingering when teaching.
- Students will be able to create their own patterns using drum sounds, R/L fingering, and/or numbers.
- Students will be able to teach movement with zil playing.

Zil Basics

Pronunciation

Let's start by talking about what finger cymbals are called. "*Zils*" is the Turkish word for finger cymbals. It rhymes with bills or chills. It is one syllable. The Arabic word for finger cymbals is *sagat*. It is pronounced "sah GAHT." Although there is no "s" on the end, sagat is plural and refers to all four-finger cymbals.

Selecting Your Zils

There are a broad range of prices and levels of quality to choose from when selecting zils. The cheap bazaar zils can cost as little as a dollar a pair. The expensive Zildjian orchestral instruments can cost more than $80 a pair. Generally, the difference in price is related to sound quality and quality of materials used in their construction.

Different metals and blend of metals are used in zil construction. Cheaper metals and blends that do not produce a sound that resonate well after the zil is struck should be avoided.

Lightweight, thin metals also tend to produce flat sounds. Less expensive zils will go out of tune faster than high quality ones too, so keep that in mind when considering which zils to buy. When purchasing zils, it is true that you get what you pay for.

Different sizes also produce different sounds. Smaller zils tend to be higher pitched and not as loud. Larger zils tend to be deeper in tone and very loud. Consider your performing environment when deciding how big you want your zils to be, but also experiment with several sizes. People with smaller hands tend to do better with smaller zils. People with larger hands find that it's easier to control larger zils.

The shape of the zil affects the ring tone and how easy they are to play. Zils with a rounded dome have more resonance (lingering sound after being struck). This is generally considered desirable. The more rim space (flat area) the zil has, the easier it is to strike. A balance of both dome and rim space is usually desirable. The greater degree of slant there is from the edge of the dome to the outer rim, the higher the pitch and the lower the overtones.

It's common in Egypt for the musician to play zils of intentionally different tones that are in harmony with each other. This is usually achieved by using zils of different sizes on each hand. It is not achieved by using zils that were purchased as a pair and one or more have gone out of tune.

When your zils are out of tune with each other, it's time to get another pair. They do not last indefinitely. Zils that do not sound musical (because the tone is dissonant) should not be played for an audience, particularly if there are musicians in the audience. Bad tone can ruin an otherwise beautiful performance. Trust me when I say that those zils that you've had for 8 years are out of tune. I don't have to hear them to know. They don't last forever. I come from a family of musicians with a wide circle of musician friends. If you heard the comments I have heard from people who know what they are talking about, you wouldn't play out of tune zils.

Securing the Zils

The zils are secured to the fingers by ½ inch or larger, flat elastic. (Smaller round elastic allows for more wobbling and less control.) Single hole zils are thought to be harder to control, so most dancers prefer to buy zils with two slits in the top. For the two-slit variety of zils, thread a piece of elastic through one slit. Wrap that around a fat dry erase marker or something that is round and about that same width. Insert the other end of the elastic through the remaining slit, so that you have two ends on the underside of the zil.

Pull the elastic tight and tie. Tie it again. Trim the edge so that the dangling elastic does not dull the sound of the zils. The zils should be tight enough to turn your finger slightly blue. If it is not this tight, redo it. Otherwise, they may fly off during your performance and hurt someone. Elastic will loosen over time, so redo your elastic on a regular basis.

If you have single-hole zils, the same procedure as above is required, but you will sew the ends of the elastic to a small button on the inside of the zil to keep the ends from being pulled through the hole.

One zil is worn on the middle finger of each hand. The other goes on the thumb of each hand. The elastic should touch just below the nail bed of each finger. Position the zils so that they can easily make contact with each other without clanging together.

Caring For Your Zils

For longer life, your zils should be stored in zil mufflers in a cloth bag in a climate-controlled environment. Metal on metal contact and extremes in temperature can reduce the tonal qualities of your zils.

Playing Your Zils

Playing Technique

When you are playing any musical instrument, you should sit or stand in posture that allows you to breathe easily through your diaphragm.

Generally speaking, you should play with your palms up. It's easier and may allow the sound to be better heard. As your hands move to frame your movements, playing with your palms up is not always going to be easier or possible. Use your judgment about this. It's not a hard and fast rule.

Zil Sounds

Zils can make many distinct sounds. The bell sound is made from striking the outer edges together and quickly pulling the edges apart. "Pulling the edges apart" doesn't mean that your hands open up as far as they can go. The further apart your fingers are, the less easy it becomes to play quickly, so just pull them apart enough to allow the zils to ring. Bringing your fingers far apart also draws attention to your hands and doesn't tend to be a very flattering look.

The "clack" is created by hitting the rims together or hitting one rim against an edge. This creates a sound that does not resonate. This is not usually a desired tone and should only be used intentionally for a specific effect.

Touching the edges together lightly without pulling them away immediately creates a small, castanet type sound.

Ringing them between your hands creates a trilling sound.

Teaching Techniques

People learn in different ways. Some students are going to pick up their zils and just start playing right away. Some will struggle with timing. Some will struggle with synchronizing movement with playing. Approaching zils in a systematic way that utilizes things that they are already familiar with (drum sounds, right hand/left hand, and numbers) should make it easier. None of these techniques teach timing, but the way they are written below, having learned rhythms before now, and hearing it on audio may help with timing.

Right- Left

Most teachers I've studied with approach zil playing by simply saying which hand to hit. "Right" means hit the zils on the right hand together. "Left" means you hit the zils on the left hand together. The hit happens when you say it happens (in other words on beat).

For faster playing, it is advisable to teach students to play with alternate hits in the beginning stage, rather than to hit on both sides. For example, when playing a triplet, it will lead to better dexterity later on if the student starts with a R-L-R pattern (or L-R-L), rather than a R-R-L (or L-L-R) pattern.

Numbers

Playing by numbers just indicates how many times to alternate hits before pausing. If the number is one, you hit once. If it's two, you hit twice. If it's three, you hit three times, and so on. Hits are always alternated between the dominant and non-dominant hand, so "3" would be R-L-R or L-R-L.

Drum Sounds

If you are playing an established rhythm with zils, you will say it and play it the same way that it is played on the drum. Dum and tek are played with the right hand. Ka is the left hand. Ayoob would be vocalized as "dum ka dum tek," and played as R-L-R-R. If it's not an established rhythm, you will drop the "dum" and simply vocalize using tek and ka in an alternating fashion. In this example "3" would be vocalized as "tek ka tek" and played as R-L-R.

The above methods give you endless creativity and freedom to do so much. Here are some examples of how to use this to get you started.

One

# of beats	1	2
Hand used	R	
Drum sound	tek	
# of hits	*	

SHAKE YOUR BOOTY

Two

# of beats	1	2
Hand used	R	L
Drum sound	tek	ka
# of hits	*	*

Three

# of beats	1	2	3	4
Hand used	R	L	R	
Drum sounds	tek	ka	tek	
# of hits	*	*	*	

Four

# of beats	1	&	a	2	&	a
Hand used	R	L	R	L		
Drum sound	tek	ka	tek	ka		
# of hits	*	*	*	*		

Five

# of beats	1	e	&	a	2	e	&	a
Hand used	R	L	R	L	R			
Drum sound	tek	ka	tek	ka	tek			
# of hits	*	*	*	*	*			

Seven

# of beats	1	e	&	a	2	e	&	a
Hand used	R	L	R	L	R	L	R	
Drum sound	tek	ka	tek	ka	tek	ka	tek	
# of hits	*	*	*	*	*	*	*	

Ayoob

# of beats	1	e	&	a	2	e	&	a
Hand used	R			L	R		R	
Drum sound	dum			ka	dum		tek	
# of hits	*			*	*		*	

Malfoof

# of beats	1	e	&	a	2	e	&	a
Hand used	R		L	R		R	L	R
Drum sound	dum		ka	tek		ka	tek	ka
# of hits	*		*	*		*	*	*

Beledi

# of beats	1	e	&	a	2	E	&	a	3	e	&	a	4	e	&	a
Hand used	R		R		R	L	R		R		R	L	R			
Drum sound	dum		dum		tek	ka	tek		dum		tek	ka	tek			
# of hits	*		*		*	*	*		*		*	*	*			

Putting Patterns Together

Once you have practiced number patterns and rhythms in isolation, practice drilling them together by mixing and matching. If speed is an issue, start with a metronome at a slow speed. Once you are comfortable at the slower speed, increase the speed.

Here are some examples of patterns you can drill.

1) Beledi; 3; 3; 7

2) Ayoob; Ayoob; 5; 5

3) 4; 5; 4; 5

4) 1; 2; 5

5) 3; 5; 3; 5

Drill different patterns to get better at changing speeds, building dexterity and confidence. When you are playing in performance, remember to match what you are playing with the music you are dancing to. Zils are musical instruments that accompany the music, so they should never overpower or compete with it. Zils are not typically considered melody instruments either, so it's rare that they should be played as melody unless you are accompanying yourself in a percussion solo.

Dancing While You Are Playing

Movement should accompany zil practice from the very beginning. Dancers should never sit while playing zils unless playing in a drum circle or accompanying someone else. Stand while you are playing at slow speeds. Once you are comfortable with the pattern or rhythm at a slow speed, walk with it. Once that is comfortable, move your arms around your body in ways that frame you as you walk. Once that is comfortable, do traveling steps while playing. Once that is comfortable, add frames to the traveling steps. Once that is comfortable, start all over with an increased tempo. Continue in that pattern until you can play comfortably at 100-120 beats per minute. Once you reach comfort with one rhythm or pattern, use that in practice and performance and start cultivating comfort with another one.

Some people say that certain patterns go with certain movements. This is a good way to start building a varied repertoire. I am an improvisational dancer at heart and prefer to play whatever I feel like playing in the moment. If you have a broad repertoire of patterns and follow what you hear, you will have this ability too. It keeps you from being locked down into specific things.

Resources for Further Study

Books

Donald, M.E., *Instructional Book and CDs for Finger Cymbals*. Available at http://www.maryellendonald.com

Donald, M.E., *Mastering Finger Cymbals*. Available at http://www.maryellendonald.com

Woods, Jenna., *The Dancing Cymbalist - How to play music with finger cymbals & dance at the same time*. (2007). Oyna Music in Motion Arts. Print.

Finger Cymbal Chapter Assessment

Submit a video or DVD of you teaching zils to a class of at least two students. The video should show you teaching while vocalizing drum sounds, R/L patterns, and counts. It should show you using rhythms and patterns and combining the three methods. The students should work up to moving while playing.

Your video/DVD should also show knowledge of all the material included in previous chapters. This doesn't mean you have to do a warm-up, give instruction on posture, etc. It means that the needs of the class should be addressed in ways that reflect the information in the previous classes as the format or needs of the student demands. Include a self-critique with ideas on what you could have done differently to improve the pieces, as well as what you think you did well.

Finger Cymbal Chapter Assessment Results

Student name:_____ Date:_____

Items are scored on a 0-5 point scale. The goal is to achieve a 3, which means that you understand the material.

0- did not attempt
1- did not demonstrate a good understanding of the material
2- demonstrated some understanding of the material
3- demonstrated an understanding of the concept
4- demonstrated good understanding of the material
5- demonstrated a mastery of the material

___ explained rhythms and patterns using drum sounds
___ explained rhythms and patterns using numbers
___ explained rhythms and patterns using R/L techniques
___ combined numbers and drum sounds when teaching
___ combined numbers and R/L technique when teaching
___ combined drum sounds and R/L technique when teaching
___ created her own patterns using drum sounds, R/L technique, and/or numbers
___ able to teach movement while zil playing

Comments:

8 MUSICALITY

Goal: Students will be able to make dance a visual representation of the music.

Objectives:
- Students will be able to discern when the music is calling for smooth moves.
- Students will be able to hear when the music is calling for percussive moves.
- Students will be able to tell when the music is calling for traveling steps.
- Students will know when a blend of music and movement is appropriate.
- Students will be able to react to intricacies of sound, such as pitch change and intensity.
- Students will know when to enter during a piece of music.

Music Interpretation

"Musicality" is the degree to which you flow with the music. There are many elements to music and many ways in which it can be interpreted. The wonderful thing about musicality is that no two people will express it in exactly the same way. Each dancer brings her own divine essence to the song that makes it unique, and when it's on, it's on. When it's off, it's not easy for someone who understands music to watch.

In my opinion, musicality is one of the most important parts of learning to belly dance. If you can't move in such a way that compliments the music, then you are not dancing. You are just doing steps in sequence. Perhaps your movement has some emotional meaning to you. Maybe it's very athletic or even artistic, but if it's not related to the music, it's like watching a subtitled movie. It's possible to get into it, but somehow the actors are never in sync with the audio.

We have laid the foundation. I am going to break down parts of music to help you understand it. If you have never had this type of instruction before, you will be delighted by how much it improves your enjoyment of the music, the dance, and your ability to express yourself.

Smooth

Smooth sounds are those that flow seamlessly without any hard breaks. When a violin is played with a bow, it produces a smooth sound. A flute or ney also produces a smooth sound. Often smooth sounds are airy.

Smooth moves are those that have no beginning and no end. They also flow seamlessly. Examples are hip circles, undulations, and amis. When you think of metaphors for smooth sounds and moves, things like chocolate, silk, brandy, and velvet might come to mind.

Percussive

Any sound that starts and stops abruptly is percussive. Drums make percussive sounds. If a violin is plucked with the fingers rather than played with a bow, that produces a percussive sound, because it starts and stops abruptly. Anything that is plucked produces a percussive sound. Short bursts of sound are also percussive, so if you have an instrument like a violin, which is played with a bow in a short burst of sound, that would also be percussive. Other examples of instruments that make percussive sounds are the oud and kanoun. However, you can see that qualities of sound are not determined purely by the type of instrument that makes the sound.

Percussive movements are those that also start and stop abruptly, like a hip shimmy, shoulder shimmy, head slide, and chest drop. When you hear percussive sounds, they should be paired with percussive movements. Words like "pop," "snap," and "bump" are often used to describe percussive movements.

Travel

Traveling sounds are those that make the body want to move from place to place. They have a feeling of movement. Some people hear movement in everything. If this is you, then try to distinguish the subtle differences in quality of sound. What sounds *more* like travel than everything else? That will be the part that you travel to.

When you hear traveling music, move! Not just in place, but from place to place. If the traveling music goes on for a while, vary the types of movement that you are doing.

Here are some examples of traveling steps:

Arabic undulation

big stroke little stroke

grapevine

step-together-step (chassé)

glide

I also put spins and turns into the category of "traveling steps" because they move in space and the musical quality is similar.

Layered Sounds

We just talked about isolating sounds into smooth, percussive, or travel feelings, but in reality, most sounds are layered. There can be smooth travels or percussive travels. There can be songs with smooth melodies overtop percussive rhythms. So what you decide to interpret is really up to you. Just pick the sound that stands out to you and sell it. If you sell it, your audience will hear it the way that you do, because you make the music visual.

When Aziz was still performing and teaching professionally, he taught a workshop for me. He danced to a song I had heard a million times before, but his interpretation picked up *so* many intricacies of the song that I had never heard before that I experienced that song in a totally different way. That's when I started to become turned on by Egyptian style dancing. When you understand musicality, you begin to be able to do that. You bring your audience into the performance experience with you so that they can experience the music and movement through you. It's a beautiful thing.

Here are some examples of layered movements:

grapevine shimmy (percussive travel)

snake arm glide (smooth travel)

undulation with hip shimmy (smooth/percussive)

hip shimmy with a hip circle (percussive/smooth)

The Entrance

If you are starting your performance from an offstage position, you need music to carry you onto the stage. Not all pieces of music give you a way to do this musically, so choose appropriately. You are "on" from the moment you are visible. It's a lot harder to make a statement if you just walk out and pose. It can be done, but it takes a lot more thinking, talent, and effort to pull off that type of entrance.

In Classical Egyptian music, it is common to have a l-o-n-g entrance. This was traditionally done to build up excitement and expectation. (American audiences frequently do not understand this, so use this type of entrance at your own risk.) You know that this is an entrance piece because it sounds like the start of a circus or something equally spectacular. You can almost see the spotlights on the stage. The music builds to a crescendo and BAM! There is the dancer.

Even when I have explained this to people, they sometimes still want to enter in the wrong place. What you are listening for is the "ta da!" and the traveling music. You generally don't slink out on an entrance. You don't shimmy out. You walk. You glide. You travel. In order to be with the music on this, you have to wait until the piece gets to the traveling music.

If you are using pop music, you may not have the big "ta da" but you are still waiting for the traveling cue to come out. Sometimes that will coincide with the first note. Sometimes you will have to wait a while.

If the first piece of music in your set does not have an entrance, use another piece of music. You can only dance what the music gives you. If it's not in the music, don't force it.

Don't enter over and over in the same set. The entrance is your time to say, "Hello! I am here! You're here. Let's get this party started!" It's generally ineffective to do that more than once. Even if you could make your music do that, it's probably not the best idea. If you think you need to go offstage, and then back on (to remove a veil or zils, for example), you may wish to figure out another way of doing that than leaving and returning. It breaks the flow of the show and your connection with your audience.

Dancing to the Melody

The melody is the part of the song that you would sing if there were words. So if the melody was being played by a saxophone, and the words were, "I adore you. I miss the sound of your voice. Why did you have to leave me?" You could interpret that emotionally. Your body and face could show that angst of not being with your beloved. That means you are probably not dancing like an Energizer Bunny and smiling at everyone. Your energy is probably internally directed and your face should be emotive.

In contrast, if you are dancing to another instrumental and the unsung words are, "Let's party tonight because tomorrow we face another hard day…" You could reflect that in your face and body. Your energy will be much more extroverted and your body language should be livelier.

Be careful with this one because many Arab songs sound happy, but the lyrics really reflect something else. Unless you are happy that your lover left you, it probably isn't consistent to have your face reflect otherwise. How much difference does it really make? It depends on whether or not you dance for natives and how much you care. If your audience is American, they won't know the difference. They will only know how the song sounds. Since they can't understand the lyrics and they sound happy, as far as they are concerned, it's consistent.

The second word of caution is to be aware that the melody is expressed by the words, the voice, *and* the lead instrument. When you are dancing to the melody, you can be dancing to any one of those. Be sure you know which one you are following when you choose to dance to the melody. Usually they are complimentary, but not always.

The Rhythm

The rhythm is the underlying beat. Some rhythms frequently used in Middle Eastern dance are Malfouf, Masmoudi, Karsilama, and Chifti-telli. The rhythm is usually created by percussion instruments. Unless you are dancing a drum solo, you usually will not be interpreting the drum. There are times when this is appropriate, however. For example, if you are dancing to a Saidi piece and the music suddenly shifts so that the drums come in with a powerful Saidi rhythm, you aren't going to ignore that. You will dance to it, but it will generally transition to something else. You won't continue to dance to the rhythm all the way through the song.

The same is true for a Chifti-telli. A Chifti-telli often starts with a drum playing that rhythm. The dancer can begin interpreting that, but usually something else will happen over the top of that that takes the lead. Where the music leads, you follow.

If someone taught you that you are supposed to always dance to the rhythm, they are not doing Middle Eastern dance. An Arab would probably say that you can't hear the music. Middle Eastern music has a high degree of complexity. Arabs enjoy when you express that. If you are dancing with only one dimension and can only follow the drum, you are not as enjoyable as you could be if you created a relationship to all the music. So follow the rhythm when it is in the forefront, but otherwise allow it to remain in the background, supporting you as it is intended to do.

Dancing to the Voice

Dancing to the voice is similar to dancing to the melody except that you are targeting the emotion, rather than the words. The voice is usually in tune with the words, but sometimes it can be doing something totally different from the instruments. If you remain true to the emotional quality of the voice, you are on track. If it sounds like a party, be lively. If it sounds like longing, show that. Whatever you decide to interpret, it should be clear. Anyone watching you should be able to tell that you are dancing to the voice. Just pick what you are interpreting and sell it. You have many options.

Interpreting the Mood

This is similar to interpreting the voice. Even if there are no lyrics, (not just that there is no one singing, but that the song actually has no words. Arabs will often break out into song when an instrumental version of a song with lyrics is playing) there is still a mood. There are some great instrumentals that move through very powerful moods and emotions. They would make incredible dance pieces, but only if the mood matches the movement of the body. If the movement were to contradict the mood, it would definitely detract from the piece. The more powerful the piece of music, the more important it is to blend sight and sound.

If you are not sure what the mood is, close your eyes. Listen, and ask yourself how does this piece make you feel? The answer may be different for different people, but as long as you can make others feel what you feel, it's right.

Be aware that it is not common to interpret only the mood in Middle Eastern dance unless the piece is a theater piece. Songs like "The Feeling Begins" from *The Last Temptation of Christ* are mood pieces. It certainly can be danced to, but it was created for background. It was created to set a mood. It belongs in a theater or in a setting where it can be appreciated for what it is.

Interpreting a Pitch Change

When I talk about a pitch change, I am saying that the notes either move up or down the musical scale. If a scale goes C, D, E, (or mi, fa, so), then a move upward would be F, G, A (or la, ti, do). A move downward would be B, A, G (or re, do, ti). Another way to state this is that the tone gets either higher or lower.

You may chose to dance through this, but if you decide to dance to it, be sure that your body in some way reflects the direction of the pitch change. A change upward should indicate a move upward, like a height change up or a hip moving up. A pitch change downward should coincide with a height change downward, or something like a hip drop downward.

This is a subtlety that is for more intermediate to advanced students. Once you start showing your musical expertise by interpreting pitch changes, you really show a oneness with your music. This may seem like a stupid little thing, but trust me. It makes a difference to Arabs and to music aficionados. If they see you moving down when the pitch is moving up, it is the type of thing that can just feel wrong. They may not be able to tell you why it feels wrong, but it can be picked up intuitively.

Interpreting the Instruments

A good teacher should be able to identify instruments by the sounds that are typically found in Middle Eastern music. This will help her define the country of origin, keep her dance style true to the country of origin, help her improvise on the fly, and educate her students to do the same.

Here are some instruments commonly found in Middle Eastern music.

Violin - The violin can be either played with a bow, which produces long, sustained sounds, or plucked with the fingers. When it is producing smooth sounds, dance using smooth movements. When it is producing the short, abrupt sounds that come from plucking, dance using percussive movements.

Flute/ney - The sounds produced by a flute or ney are generally smooth, so the movements used should be smooth as well. Examples are hip circles, figure eights, undulations, and veil work.

Kanoun - A kanoun is a stringed instrument that looks like a zither or a harp. It is played by plucking with the fingers. Any time an instrument is plucked, it produces a sound that starts and stops abruptly; therefore, a kanoun should be interpreted as a percussive instrument. Usually the plucking is very fast and results in a shimmying type of sound.

Oud - The oud is a stringed instrument that looks like a lute. It is plucked with the fingers, thus producing a sound that starts and stops suddenly (percussive).

Drum - Of course the drum produces percussive sounds and should be accompanied by percussive movements. Other percussive instruments, such as the tar, riq, and finger cymbals are interpreted the same way.

Accordion - The accordion is a little tricky because it can be interpreted as either a smooth sound or a percussive sound, depending upon how it is played. It is a bit earthier in style, however, and this should be reflected in your interpretation. Flat footed, folkloric style movements tend to be most appropriate when you hear this instrument.

Rababa - This is a stringed instrument that can be played and interpreted like a violin. It is much earthier, however, and should be interpreted as such. It is associated with more Beledi styles of music.

Mizmar - This woodwind is capable of making long, sustained sounds, as well as short, choppy sounds. It is similar to an oboe. It is very folkloric and should be interpreted with earthy overtones.

Interpreting the Intensity of the Music

The intensity of your dance should almost always be a reflection of the intensity of the music. When I am talking intensity, I am asking how much space does the music take up in the air? Does it reach the back of the room? Does it vibrate throughout the room? Or does it whisper? Does it reverberate through your bones? Or does it barely touch you? It can brush by you, while still impacting you deeply, so don't be fooled by softness of tone.

When I ask these questions, I am trying to get you to listen. Listen to the power of the music, the energy of the music. Is it big? Or is it small? Is it introverted? Or extroverted? How does it feel? Many times, the intensity coincides with the instrumentation, so there is a little hint for you. If the whole orchestra is playing loudly, the energy is usually big. A big feeling cries for large movements, moving through a large amount of space with extroverted energy. If you have a solo instrument playing quietly, that is small energy. That can be represented by internal energy and small movements. Small energy usually doesn't move much in space.

Showing the Musical Structure

Recall from chapter four that music has structure. If the structure is ABA, the second time you get to A, it should resemble what you did the first time, because the music is the same or a variation of the first time. This is both musical and expected in Middle Eastern dance.

If you have a motif (a repeating theme or idea), that should also be reflected in your musical interpretation.

In western dance, it is acceptable for the dancer to be considered the "lead" instrument or the melody, while the music supports her. Western dance also frequently contrasts the music. Middle Eastern dance is different. It compliments or reflects the music, but does not compete with it, lead it, or contrast it.

Call and Reply

"Call and reply" happens frequently in Arab music. A phrase plays, and then is "answered." The first time it might be with a single instrument. The second time it might be echoed by the entire orchestra. Or the first time could be instrumental and the second time is with voice. (It could be visualized like this XXXXXXXX, xxxxxxxx—the same, but different). Recognizing this pattern gives you a great way to improvise on the fly. If you know that X happened once, you are better able to copy it the second time it comes around.

So what does your body do with this? First, you want to interpret the instrumentation. If the entire phrase is percussive, both repetitions of the phrase should be percussive in nature. Then think about the energy. If the "call" is big and the "reply" is small, your interpretation should reflect that. So the energy the first time should be bigger and more outward, and the energy the second time should be smaller and more introverted. The movements that you chose to do can either be the same or different. For example, you could do a big hip shimmy, followed by a vibration, or you could do a hip shimmy the first time, followed by a shoulder shimmy.

"Rule of Four"

Arab music frequently makes use of the "rule of four." What this means is, if you hear a phrase, you will hear it four times in a row. This is great when it happens during an improvisational drum solo. If you miss the change the first time, you have three more tries to get it just right!

When you get blocks of music like this that are the same, don't overlook that. Music provides the structure for dance, so if something repeats musically, it should resemble that pattern in dance. For example, if you dance ABcdEFg the first time, you may wish to do abCDefG the second time, so that you are still reflecting the music, while keeping things fresh and entertaining.

Picking Out Accents

Quite often the music will include little accents that add richness to the audience's experience when the dancer interprets them. Accents create great opportunities to throw in something special—especially when the piece of music is repetitive. The accents won't be missed if you choose to dance through them, but they will definitely be noticed if you use them. The interpretation of the accent will depend on what the accent is. If you decide to dance to an accent, make sure that you have enough space to easily transition back to the main body of the piece, so that the dancing doesn't look rushed or jumbled. You can often do this by incorporating a pause or slowing the tempo down.

Be careful of interpreting every accent. Too much accenting is like having too much pepper in your lasagna. A little goes a long way in adding spice. Too much overwhelms. I once saw a contestant perform a piece solely dancing to the accents. I am sure she thought she was being clever, but it looked and felt very strange. Balance is what makes traditional and innovative things blend well together.

Common Musicality Mistakes

Changing Qualities In the Middle of a Musical Phrase

A "phrase" is a piece of music that fits within the larger body of music. It can be short or long. It is recognizable as a phrase, because when it changes, the music obviously moves to something else. For example, if I am listening to a piece of music that starts with a drum roll for two counts of eight before a violin picks up the melodic lead, that little bit of drum roll is a "phrase."

Each phrase has a definite quality of sound. Your movement should match that quality of sound and be sustained for as long as the phrase lasts. In the above example, you should be doing something with a percussive quality for two counts of eight. You are not going to move from percussive to smooth on the "five." You are not going to start traveling on the second count of "one." You are usually going to sustain that percussive quality of movement for the entire length of the phrase. Why? To do otherwise is to go against the music. When the music stops, you stop. When the phrase stops, you change to something else. Not before.

This doesn't mean that you have to shimmy in place the entire time. It just means that the quality of sound should be a sustained, percussive movement. It could be a shoulder shimmy for eight counts, followed by a hip shimmy for eight counts. It could be a traveling choo choo shimmy the entire time. It could be a shimmy that moves from the hips to the shoulders to the head and back down. It doesn't really matter, as long as the *quality* of sound is sustained for as long as the phrase lasts.

Over Dancing the Music

When I've seen dancers over dancing the music, it is usually because the dancer wants to show off her "amazing" technical ability. This is a bad example of musicality. Doing things just because you can is not a good way to express the music. Dance is a relationship between music and movement. If you ignore the music, the movement is not showcased in the most impressive light. Remember, if it's not in the music, it shouldn't be in the dance. A better way to handle the desire to showcase your talent is to chose a piece of music that is better suited to displays of technical or athletic ability.

If you design a choreography by writing down movements and putting everything you can think of into the choreography for the sake of variety, you are probably over dancing the music. If you dance non-stop and do every move you can think of, you are probably over dancing the music. If your piece is highly technical all the way through with lots of layers and challenging transitions, you are probably over dancing the music. Even the most technical pieces of music have places to rest and breathe.

Keep in mind that subtlety is a skill, just as theatrics, technicality, artistry, and acrobatics are skills. When the dancer can speak with more than one voice (example: dance with fire then move to ice, or spring out with energy then bring the energy down to a whisper), she has more tools with which to captivate her audience. She can broaden her repertoire tremendously. When she can use all that the music gives her, she is truly an artist.

So dance to what the music gives you. No more. No less. Remember, your movement is an expression of the music. If you are over the top, you take away from the enjoyment of the music and the visual magic that you are trying to create. If you give your audience less than the music is giving, you are a distraction to the ear. Your show should be a compliment to the music. When you join with the music, the result should be greater than the dance or the song could be on its own.

Further Hints on Musicality

If the music gives you the opportunity to stop, use it. It's a great time for people to take pictures. It gives you the chance to catch your breath. It adds variety to your performance. Dramatic pauses can refocus the energy back on you.

Dance with your whole body, including your face. In fact, practice this. It may seem phony, but if you get used to emoting while dancing, it becomes habit. It frees you to express yourself in the moment.

Be conscious of your performance space when choosing a piece of music. If you are on a stage, pick a piece of music that will play well on stage, with the audience far away. If you are in a more intimate setting, pick music that isn't too big, because you won't have the space to do it justice. Big music looks overdone in a small space. You won't be able to travel much, so that can look cramped if you reduce the scale. Don't do a theater piece in a restaurant.

Understanding and working with the music is what makes dance dance. Without it, it's as entertaining as watching someone do drills. The blend of sight, sound, and emotion makes the experience whole. If the information in this chapter is new to you, play with it. Work with interpreting instruments, then qualities of sound, then interpreting the voice. This will enhance your choreography and improvisation tremendously. Not to mention the audience's enjoyment of your performance.

Authentic Middle Eastern dance does not separate music from movement—period. If you are teaching and performing a fusion form of belly dance, which relies more on counting, acrobatics, theatrics, or some other element, that's fine. Having musical knowledge will expand your ability to teach and perform even fusion forms of belly dance.

Some people feel overwhelmed by having to listen to everything, and then figure out what to do with it. Other people feel that doing only what the music gives limits their expression. If you or your students are in the latter category, you can vary your presentation by creating exciting combinations, utilizing layered movements, or incorporating dynamics.

For example, the first student may hear smooth for eight counts, followed by a traveling smooth for eight counts, then more smooth. She may choose to interpret this by doing a hip circle for 8 counts, then a glide with a chest circle in a circle around center stage, then undulate to the right for 4 counts, then left for four counts. That would be an appropriate interpretation of what she heard.

The second student may hear the same music as small and smooth with an underlying tremble to it. The second phrase is big and smooth, with a sense of movement underneath that (travel). Then it changes to a joyous feeling of anticipation, which is also carried by smooth sounds. She may choose to interpret this by side to side swaying mayas with her eyes closed for the first eight counts, followed by a bold ¾ shimmy walk which takes up a lot of space. As she performs this part, her eyes are wide open, her face is lit up, and she is looking boldly out to the audience. Then she spins for 4 counts and blends it into a big hip circle, which she frames by bringing her arms across her chest as she bends towards the audience.

Both dancers heard the same music. The beginner who is just struggling to interpret it well can focus on matching moves to music. The more advanced dancer can use all her powers of communication to make her body speak what the music is saying. The level of your students doesn't matter. They can always dance musically.

Suggestions for How to Teach Musicality

Some people will naturally understand the concept of musicality. They will be able to hear the nuances of sound and understand conceptually how to make that visible, if not know how to do it in the body. Others will need a lot of instruction. One way to make this happen is to approach it in three steps: Observe, Describe, Participate.

Observe means to experience the music through the eyes, ears, taste, touch, and scent. What image does this music call to mind? Does it bring to mind the image of a little girl twirling in a ballooning dress? Or maybe it's more like a horse running wildly with his nostrils flaring. What does it sound like? Rainfall? A scream in the night air? Building intensity? How about a taste? Could this music be as smooth as warm chocolate on the tongue? Or bitter like bile? Does it bring to mind a feeling sensation? Feelings can be emotional feelings or actual tactile sensations. Does this music feel like falling in love? Or maybe it feels like velvet against the skin. Does it bring to mind a scent? Does it make you recall the lingering scent of jasmine? Or spilled beer after a night of dancing and partying? Observing what senses are stimulated by the music can help to jump start a stalled dancer.

Describe means to give words to the senses that are experienced. By verbalizing the sensations, it starts to solidify the image. It starts to create mental pictures of what movements go with those words.

Participate means to become the image. The music carries you. All you have to do is pair your physical response to the sensations it creates. It's a meeting of technical skill with artistry.

Have the class observe, and then describe a short musical phrase. Allow them to participate in creating dances that create a visual representation of what they have observed and described. Let them comment on what they saw and felt. Feedback creates an opportunity for them to learn whether or not their interpretation was received as intended. As they become more comfortable with this and the idea that dance is a visual representation of the music, their musicality should improve.

Musicality Cheat Sheet

Here is a cheat sheet of things you can interpret that can help you get through a piece of music musically.

- Smooth sounds
- Percussive sounds
- Traveling sounds
- Blended sounds
- Specific instrument quality (including voice)
- Loudness or softness
- Internal or external energy
- A specific emotional quality
- Speed (fast or slow)
- Space (takes up a little or a lot)
- Intensity
- Voice
- Melody
- Rhythm
- Repetitions
- Motif
- Accents
- Pauses

Musicality Chapter Assessment

Submit a video of you teaching an entire class of at least two people for at least thirty minutes (but no more than one hour). This could be a class on musicality or simply a class that demonstrates your intellectual understanding of musicality, as well as your ability to demonstrate it. You can use improvisation, choreography, drills, or whatever can best illustrate that you understand how to interpret music. Make sure that both you and the students can be seen and heard. The video/DVD should include:

- an entrance
- appropriate use of smooth moves
- appropriate use of percussive moves
- appropriate use of traveling steps
- appropriate use of blended sounds
- interpretation of intricacies of sound

Your video should also show knowledge of material included in the previous chapters.

Include a self-critique with ideas on what you could have done differently to improve the class, as well as what you think you did well.

Remember: I am not expecting perfection. Don't be afraid to stretch yourself. Attempt something that you are unsure about. Don't be afraid of feedback. The more you challenge yourself in your assessment, the greater your potential to learn.

Musicality Chapter Assessment Results

Student name:_____   Date:_____

Items are scored on a 0-5 point scale. The goal is to achieve a 3, which means that you understand the material.

0- did not attempt
1- did not demonstrate a good understanding of the material
2- demonstrated some understanding of the material
3- demonstrated an understanding of the material
4- demonstrated a good understanding of the material
5- demonstrated a mastery of the material

___ can execute an appropriate entrance
___ can pair smooth sounds to smooth movements
___ can pair percussive sounds to percussive movements
___ can pair traveling sounds to traveling movements
___ can appropriately layer movements
___ demonstrates an understanding of intricacies of sound

Comments: (May include observations on all previous chapters).

9 CHOREOGRAPHY

Goal: Students will have an understanding of how to create simple and intermediate level choreographies for individuals and groups.

Objectives:
- Students will be able to create beginner and intermediate level choreography.
- Students will be able to create choreography for a group and a single individual.
- Students will be able to create choreography that follows the music.
- Students will be able to demonstrate variety in use of time, space, energy, and form.
- Students will be able to map out the music on paper to reflect the musical form.

Choreography

The information in this chapter is intended to be an overview of the art of choreography, but keep in mind that choreography is not authentic to Middle Eastern dance—particularly group choreography. You are free to employ a western sense of what it means to choreograph, but know that if you stray outside of the goal of making the music visible, it's no longer "authentic." That's okay, because sometimes you have to move outside of authenticity in order to make your dance work. For example, if you strive to put a group on stage, you must choreograph. It would be chaos otherwise. If your goal is to put folkloric dances on stage, you must choreograph or else you risk being incredibly boring, as folklore is extremely repetitious by nature. So even if you are teaching authentic Middle Eastern dance, it's important to have the skill of choreography.

Choreography is an important teaching skill as well. Choreography can provide you with a way to put all your ideas together in a cohesive package. For example, if your lesson focuses on learning specific combinations, using those combinations in a choreography is a good way to demonstrate how to use the combinations in a meaningful way. If your lesson is about teaching dynamics, putting dynamics changes in a choreography can show students how they work within a performance piece.

In order to do choreography well, you must understand musicality (the visual representation of the sounds), which we talked about in chapter seven. You should also understand musical form (chapter five), which is the overall structure of a song. Elements of dance and how they work together should also be explored. Once you have all those pieces, you are ready to choreograph! In this chapter, we will review musical form and elements of dance separately and then put them together.

Musical Form

Every piece of music has a structure or plan. Some forms are simple and easy to grasp. Some are more difficult and require dissection to understand. Some are familiar, so they will be easier to work with. Others will be new to you.

Once you are able to understand the pieces of the musical structure or form, it will be a lot easier for you to hear and work with the parts. If you can understand the whole structure of a piece of music, it will be a lot easier for you to formulate a dance, because dance should always follow and compliment the music.

Here are some definitions that can help you understand and explain musical elements:

Introduction

Not all songs have an introduction. If there is an introduction, it is at the beginning of the song and does not usually repeat.

Verse

The verse follows the introduction and comes before the chorus. It is the part that is meant to be sung. When verses repeat, the melody is the same, but the words are different. An example of a song sung in verses is "Silent Night."

Refrain

The refrain is similar to a verse, but the refrain has the same words and same melody. An example of this is "Row, Row, Row Your Boat." The words simply repeat over and over.

Bridge

The bridge is a transitional passage that connects two parts of a song. This usually happens only once and is situated in the middle to end of a song. Not all songs have a bridge. In Middle Eastern music, it is not uncommon for the bridge to be the same or similar to the introduction. However, in western music, the bridge is never the same as the introduction.

Phrase

A phrase is a piece of the music, commonly four to eight measures, that makes sense together, but does not form a complete melody. This may make more sense if you think of it as being similar to a written phrase, such as, "Once upon a time…" It's not a complete sentence, but it does represent a clear idea. The musical phrase could be expressed as ending where the comma in a sentence would be. Just listen for the pause. The opening words of "A b c d e f g…" from the "Alphabet Song" would be an example of a phrase. The second phrase of course would be, "H i j k l m n o p."

Be careful about plopping movement phrases (or combinations) into musical phrases. The two are not necessarily compatible. A movement phrase should be created with the musical accompaniment in mind. It should match in intensity, feeling, and image. It should not be matched together on the basis of having the same number of counts in the phrase.

Form

Form can be visually expressed by using written notation (visual). You can hear the form with your ears (auditory). You can express it through the body (kinesthetic). Be sure to take a multi-modal approach when teaching choreography, so that your students with different learning modalities can grasp the material.

Describing the Form

There are two widely used ways of describing the form. The first way involves labeling with letters. The second way uses names that describe an established, common way that music is put together.

Labeling with Letters

Labeling with letters involves chopping up the music into parts and designating them with letters. For example, the first part would be called A. If the second part is similar to A, but not exactly, you could label that A' (called "A prime"). I label it A2. Either way, there should be some sort of designation to show that the first A and the second A are very similar, but not identical.

When the divided parts are different, you just use the next letter. So the next section that is different from A would be called B. The next part that is different from A and B could be called C, and so on.

Knowing when to divide music into a new part comes from listening to the changes and differences. Sometimes the changes will be obvious. If the tempo changes drastically, that could be a signal that you are moving to a new part. Sometimes the change will come from the melody. Other times it could be a change in harmony (Middle Eastern music uses little to no harmony), texture (meaning the bigness or smallness of a piece, solo voice, multiple voices, voices at different octaves, etc), or tonal quality (meaning quality of sound- for example, breathy vs. clear).

You could also think of dividing points as full sentences. If you put phrases together that make a complete sentence, you probably have created the "right" block that should be labeled with its own letter.

A

Music with the label "A" obviously implies simple songs. These songs have one short section without a lot of changes. Great examples of this are found in children's nursery rhymes, such as *Jack and Jill*, *Mary Had a Little Lamb*, and *Little Bo Peep*.

A A' A"

Music with the form A, A, A repeats over and over. The verses can be made different by having a soloist sing/play, then the chorus/orchestra. The first A may be a soloist, followed by the melody with harmony. If any changes are made, they are not significant. Many church hymns use this structure. "America the Beautiful" is another example of the A A' A" pattern.

A B A" B A" B' or A B A' B C B'

This is a popular form used for pop music. KNOW THIS ONE! You will see it A LOT! This pattern signifies that you have one block followed by a different block. The third block sounds a lot like the first, but is not identical. The fourth block is the same as the second. The fifth block sounds similar to the first and third blocks, but not identical. The final block is similar to the second and fourth blocks.

To put all this into perspective, go to www.youtube.com and enter "Viva Las Vegas just dance," in the search bar. You should get several videos of the Just Dance cartoon choreography for "Viva Las Vegas." Click on one of them and watch it. Follow along with the notes below.

"Viva Las Vegas" starts out with a section during which the dancer is getting ready to dance, but isn't performing yet. I call that the "Introduction." There is no singing here. This lasts for four counts of eight. There are five other blocks.

A is four counts of eight. This is the part when he's riding the horse, followed by a twist.
B lasts for four counts of eight. This is when he starts shooting out to the side and in front.
C is two counts of eight. This is when he's singing, "Viva Las Vegas," and his arms go out to the side.
D is four counts of eight. This is when he is walking side to side with his arms going in and out.
E is only eight counts. This is when he shoots the ground.
F is the finale and lasts for four counts of eight. He uses this to finish the routine.

The whole blocked dance looks like this:
ABC
ABC
D
E
ABC
F

Labeling with Names

Here are some examples of musical forms that are commonly used and are already named:

Canon

A canon is an imitation of a melodic line. This usually takes place by a different voice, instrument, or pitch. The second line starts after the first. The letter designation for this pattern is A A' A".

Round

A round is a canon that uses different voices singing the same words over and over again. An example of this would be "Frere Jacque" or "Three Blind Mice." The letter designation for a round is A A A.

Rondo

A rondo describes a pattern of music in which one section repeats and a new section follows (ABA, ABACA, or ABACABA). Examples of songs are Bach's *E Major Violin Concerto* and the last movement of Beethoven's *Piano Sonata, Op 13*.

There are many, many, many more ways that music can be formed. There are many popular forms that have names. I don't want to bog you down with learning all of them. The important thing is to know how to hear the changes, so that you can structure your choreographies in a way that flows and follows the music. I've taken many classes in which the choreographers create dance phrases that go with one musical phrase. Then the movement phrase repeats to a different musical phrase, or starts in the middle of the original phrase! Talk about confusing! Mistakes like these can be avoided by writing out, thinking about, and listening to the musical form.

Elements of Choreography

Time

Timing refers to how fast, slow, and long-lasting a movement is. Timing also refers to how movements are phrased and accented. It should always be clear what rhythm the dancer is following. Movement should always be clear, not mushy. There should be a moderate amount of variation in timing. Too much, and the observer is overwhelmed. Too little, and the observer can become bored.

The music will usually dictate your timing. If the music is fast, your dancing is fast. If the notes are long and sustained, your movement will mirror that most of the time. However, if the musical patterns don't have a lot of variety, you may wish to slow the tempo down to half time or double it in places.

If you are choreographing for a group, you may wish to make use of different parts of the music for different dancers. For example, group A is interpreting a slow, smooth part of the music that overlays fast percussion, which is being danced by group B.

Space

Patterns of movement on the floor should be created to flow with the music, make the music visible, maximize use of space, and create harmony. There should be balance between too much movement and too little. If the choreography is created for a group, spacing and movement should make the best use of the number of people involved. They should neither be too close together, nor too far apart.

Space may be maximized by utilizing high and low space, such as having some dancers on the ball of their feet while others are doing floor work. A solo dancer could also alternate between using high and low space. Keep in mind, however, that "maximizing space" does not necessarily mean, "using the most space." It means using the space you have wisely. An emotional piece that draws you in might best be illustrated with little traveling movement that edges toward the back of the stage, for example.

Another way to maximize use of space is through various travel patterns. "Flocking" is when an ensemble moves from one shape to another, such as going from a "V" shape to a circle or line. Changing visual patterns can keep your dance interesting.

The direction of travel should be such that the audience has the best view of the movement, unless there is a logical reason to do otherwise. The travel patterns should be varied using linear, rounded, symmetrical, and asymmetrical patterns. Level changes should also be used to maximize the space closest to the floor and above the dancer's heads. The choreography should also take into consideration where the audience is. Is it on three sides? Is the stage recessed?

Use of space also considers the energy dynamic and psychological impact of where the dancer is on stage. The most powerful point on stage is center stage, because everyone can see you there. It's also a placement that indicates the "here and now" and immediate action. As you move closer to the audience, this demands the audience's attention, because you begin to encroach on their space. This may be too intimate and strong for a belly dance performance and should be considered before moving into this space. The back of the stage is a great place for intimate and quiet things to take place. Caution is needed, however, because you can also lose contact with your audience if you feel too far away.

When dancing with a group, consider putting the larger dancers toward the back and to the left, while smaller dancers are to the front and to the right in a diagonal. This will lessen the impact of size disparity and make the group look more similar. Also consider the use of personal space when dancing with a group. It's common and considerate to choreograph with personal space requirements in mind, but it may be more beguiling to the audience's eyes to violate those norms and make the space more or less intimate.

Energy

Energy refers to the quality of movement. Words like floating, heavy, and sharp describe the energy of movement. You can vary the texture of your choreography simply by giving different energy to different parts of the piece. Here are some examples:

Climax - building energy, usually at the end, that stands out from the rest of the piece

Collapsing - sudden release of movement

Contrasting - using different energies at the same time

Counterpointe - using opposite energies at the same time

Dynamics - creating variations of movement through the use of energy, time, or space

Sustain - hanging in space before collapsing

Form

Dance either follows a narrative or a pattern. If it's a narrative, it follows a story. There may be an introduction, conflict, climax, and resolution. Meanings and concepts may be explored throughout the piece.

If the dance follows a pattern, the movement follows a pattern. It may be abstract or orderly. It may be based on the form of the music. For example, if the musical pattern is ABAB, the dance pattern will also be ABAB. If there is a call and reply, a soloist may perform, followed by the chorus, to demonstrate a small sound followed by a big sound. If there is a canon, one person may do phrase A, followed by another doing the same thing but starting at a different time.

Form in dance is used the same way as it is in music. It is simply a way to organize movement in a way that compliments the music, gives the dance structure, and establishes a beginning, middle, and end.

In Middle Eastern choreography, the form is going to follow the music. If the form is AB, you have one movement phrase followed by a different movement phrase. If the form is ABA, the first movement phrase is the same as the last. The middle one is different.

This structure doesn't limit your creativity however. You still have other elements to play with that can make it interesting.

Here are some ideas to include balance and creativity:

Asymmetry - deliberately creating an imbalance for a specific effect. Famed choreographer Bob Fosse did this with brilliance! You can use asymmetry as a soloist or with a group.

Mirroring - imitating the movement of another so that it is identical when facing that person.

Quality - same movement but with a different feeling, for example a sensuous hip circle vs. a shy one.

Repetition - repeating. This can be done consecutively or throughout the piece.

Retrograde - performing a movement or phrase backward.

Rhythm - altering the pattern of beats. For example, if you had dum, dum, dum, dum (1, 2, 3, 4) for four counts, you could do dum-dum, dum-dum, dum, dum (1, and, 2, and, 3, 4) for four counts instead.

Size - making the movement or phrase smaller or larger.

Speed - making the movement or phrase faster or slower, but make sure it maintains the same size.

Staging - using a different part of the stage. For example, you did X the first time facing front and center, when you repeat it, you are on the diagonal closer to the front. Staging also includes what can be seen in the light, so what is brightly lit will feel different from what is seen in shadows.

Symmetry - balancing what happens on one side with what happens on the other side. This doesn't necessarily mean that you do X on the right and X on the left, although that is an example. You could use high space on one side and low space on the other side to create symmetry. Dancers in a line, using an even number of dancers, or dancers evenly spaced are all examples of symmetry.

Unity - established thought cohesiveness of the entire piece.

Variation - using the original theme and changing it through time, space, and energy.

Common Mistakes

Choreography is a skill quite separate from learning how to teach or dance. Most of us are not "good" choreographers, nor do we aspire to be, but it is a necessary teaching tool. You can create quite serviceable choreographies that give your students structure and teach underlying skills and concepts, but if you want to be "better," here are some common mistakes to watch out for.

Filling spaces with any old thing because you are stuck. I've done this. You have probably been tempted to do this too. These "dead spots" in your choreography will stick out, particularly if the rest of your choreography is quite good. Keep working at it until something fits well within the entire piece.

Too much symmetry. Most of the belly dance choreography I have seen is exactly this. There are two to this side and two to that side, four to the right and four to the left. There is nothing wrong with that- particularly with beginners. I actually even think that's a good thing for beginners, because it gets them relating to musical structure through their bodies and ears before their minds ever get involved. However, I believe that once you grow in dance, your choreography should grow to reflect that knowledge. At that stage, the over reliance on symmetry to achieve balance should disappear.

Imbalance in performers' ability. If your dancers are not of the same skill level, you choreograph to the weakest link. Choreographing to the strongest, or even the middle, will emphasize the deficits of those who cannot keep up. It makes the choreography unbalanced. This imbalance refers to technical as well as artistic skill.

Not taking the performance space into consideration. All choreographies cannot be performed in all spaces. If you have floor work, it is not going to be seen in a restaurant by anyone who isn't immediately surrounding you. If you are on a large stage, vibrations will probably be missed. If you are in an intimate setting, big traveling moves are going to be overwhelming. Your three-sided choreography will lose a lot if you only have audience in front of you.

Overreliance on non-dance elements. It's fantastic if you are able to consider the music, costuming, lighting, staging, and props in your performance piece, but those things are not going to carry the performance if your dancers can't perform it. Your stage, costume, or props should not outshine the dancer.

Not using enough repetition. Sometimes teachers hate repetition so much that they go over board in avoiding it. Repetition is necessary to bring the elements together. It's a natural part of music and dance, so don't avoid it. Balance it.

Putting It All Together

Choreography starts with choosing a piece of music. Think about who the performance is for, what is the music saying, where the piece will be performed, what costuming will compliment the piece, and any other consideration that may influence the choice of music.

Once you have settled on a piece, listen to it over, and over, and over. Know every nuance of it. If it has a subtle drop in energy, know where that is. If it lingers a little long in one place, remember that. Those subtle nuances are worth paying attention to.

Now that you have remembered the sound of it, create a rough visual map of the music. The rough map is to give you an idea of the form. Is it ABA? Is there a long taxim in the middle? How many times does the main theme repeat? These things will give you an idea of how complex or simple you want your piece to be.

There are many ways to make a rough map of your music. You can do this by counts, for example, "2 x 8- intro/off stage" would mean that there are two counts of eight for the introduction, which are off stage.

You could do this with symbols, for example: "2 x 8 - ~~~~(4), xxxx (4), ~~~~(4), ^^^X (4)" would mean that you have two counts of eight. The first four counts are smooth moves, the next four counts are percussive moves, the next four are smooth moves, and the final four are three counts of travel followed by one count of percussive. I just made up these symbols. Your symbols could be anything you want them to be. I'd keep it simple at this stage, however. You are just making a rough map of the music, not trying to choreograph the whole piece.

Once you have a big picture idea of what the music is doing, you may wish to further refine your rough map by blocking out phrases that repeat. Include enough notes to yourself that you have a general idea of what goes where musically, and what you want to put there for movement. There is no set way to do this, so do whatever makes sense for you.

Here is a rough map of "Youm Al Hazz" from the CD *Ya Habibi* by Al Ahram Orchestra that shows you how to put together the above ideas.

Youm Al Hazz (rough map)

Intro	8	(drums, off stage)
A	4 x 8	(keyboard, off stage)
B	4 x 8	(entrance, travel, spin)
C	4 x 8	(percussion, smooth, smooth)
B		
C		
D	4 x 8	(travel, flutes, pitch goes down at end)
B		
C		
E	16 x 8	(taxim)
A		
B		
C		last eight count is different.

Preliminary notes on my map: This a rough map so that I can see the overall structure of the piece first. This one is ABC, BCD, BDE, ABC. The last C is actually not a C, because the last eight counts of it are different, but since only the last eight counts are different, I will still call it C. (If this doesn't work for you, feel free to use your own system. The important thing is that it makes sense to you and your students.)

A is actually included in the intro, but the first eight counts don't repeat, so I wanted to separate that out. A in this piece is actually also the bridge.

The structure of the piece is pretty even. Most of the phrases are three groupings of four counts of eight. There don't appear to be any surprises.

I included the overall qualities of sound so I could get an idea of what I am working with. I want to use the taxim as an improvisational dance piece for the intermediate solo choreography., It's a good contrast to the rest of the piece and intermediates should be able to improvise there, assuming they are soloing. If it is to be a group piece, that wouldn't work.

Since the repetition of ABC is separated by two other sections, including a fairly long taxim, I will keep those two sections almost the same, with the exception of the final pose. I will use variations for B and C in the phrases of BCD and BCE to give some contrast.

When I actually write my choreography, I am going to include much more detail. Here is my beginner's version. I tend to be Spartan in my notation. If you want to include more detail, such as what the arms are doing, which foot is pointing, or which way you are turning, feel free to do so.

Youm Al Hazz (beginner version)

Intro	8	off stage
A	8	off stage
	8	off stage
	8	off stage
	8	off stage
B	8	step together step to center stage
	8	spin
	8	face left diagonal, karsilama shimmy forward and back with hip lift on the back, hip drop circle front to back
	8	spin, pose
C	8	hip drop, drop drop, pause; figure eight
	8	Yes- I-do; hip circle
	8	(other side) hip drop, drop, drop, pause; figure eight
	8	Yes- I-do; hip circle
B	8	step touch (1-2), step touch (3-4), turn (5-8)
	8	Arabic 6 (1-4) turn with hip drops in place (5-8)
	8	step touch on other side (1-2), step touch (3-4), turn (5-8)
	8	dropping O to the front diagonal (1-4) with snake arms up (5-8)
C	8	arms up r,l, r (1-4), turn (5-8)
	8	ami (1-4), maya (5-8)
	8	arms up r, l, r (1-4), turn (5-8)
	8	wrist circles down, figure eights, ami (7-8)
D	3x 8	walk (step-together-step, or step-touch) in a figure eight pattern
	8	jack knife slowly, pose
B	8	Basic Egyptian (1-4), turn (5-8)
	8	Arabic undulation turn
	8	Basic Egyptian (1-4), turn (5-8)
	8	dropping O to other side front diagonal (1-4) snake arms up (5-8)
C	8	arms up r, l, r (1-4), turn (5-8)
	8	ami (1-4), maya (5-8)
	8	arms up r, l, r (1-4), turn (5-8)
	8	wrist circles down, figure eights, ami (7-8)
E	16 x 8	taxim
A	8	head slide (6), chest drop (7, 8)
	8	shoulder shimmy (slow) (6), chest drop (7, 8)
	8	hip slide (6), pelvic drop (7, 8)
	8	ami (6), pelvic drop (7, 8)
B	8	step together step in circle
	8	spin from low to high
	8	face left diagonal, karsilama shimmy forward & back with hip lift on the back, hip drop circle front to back
	8	spin, pose

C	8	hip drop, drop, drop, while dropping, pause; figure eight
	8	shoulder shimmy with karsilama step overlay; dropping hip circle
	8	(other side) hip drop, drop, drop, pause; figure eight
	8	Yes- I-do; hip circle

Youm Al Hazz (intermediate version)

Intro	8	off stage
A	4 x 8	off stage
B	8	step together step to center stage
	8	spin from low to high
	8	face left diagonal, karsilama shimmy forward and back with hip lift on the back, hip drop circle front to back
	8	spin, pose
C	8	hip drop, drop, drop, while dropping pause; figure eight
	8	shoulder shimmy with karsilama step overlay; dropping hip circle
	8	(other side) hip drop, drop, drop while dropping, pause; figure eight
	8	shoulder shimmy with karsilama step overlay; dropping hip circle
B	8	step touch (1-2), step touch (3-4), swivel turn (5-8)
	8	Arabic 6 (1-4) turn with hip drops (5-8) in personal circle
	8	step touch on other side (1-2), step touch (3-4), swivel turn (5-8)
	8	dropping O to the front diagonal (1-4) with snake arms up (5-8)
C	8	Zoheir's hip drop (1-3), turn
	8	ami (1-4), maya (5-8)
	8	Zoheir's hip drop (1 3), turn (4)
	8	wrist circles down, figure eights, ami (7-8)
D	3x 8	walk (step-together-step, or step-touch) in a figure eight pattern
	8	jack knife slowly, pose
B	8	Basic Egyptian (1-4), swivel turn (5-8)
	8	Arabic undulation turn
	8	Basic Egyptian (1-4), swivel turn (5-8)
	8	dropping O to other side front diagonal (1-4) snake arms up (5-8)
C	8	Zoheir's hip drop (1-3), turn
	8	ami (1-4), maya (5-8)
	8	Zoheir's hip drop (1-3), turn (4)
	8	wrist circles down, figure eights, ami (7-8)
E	16 x 8	taxim
A	8	snake arm glide to right diagonal, chest drop
	8	snake arm glide to back, hip right, hip left
	8	snake arm glide to left diagonal, chest drop
	8	snake arm glide to center, head slide

B	8	step together step to center stage
	8	spin from low to high
	8	face left diagonal, karsilama shimmy forward & back with hip lift on the back, hip drop circle front to back
	8	spin, pose
C	8	hip drop, drop drop, while dropping pause; figure eight
	8	shoulder shimmy with karsilama step overlay; dropping hip circle
	8	(other side) hip drop, drop, drop while dropping, pause; figure eight
	8	shoulder shimmy with karsilama step overlay; spin, pose arms up

Resources for Further Study

Books

Blom, L.A., Chaplin, L. T., *The Intimate Act of Choreography*, University of Pittsburg Press. (1982). Print.

Ellfeldt, L., *A Primer for Choreographers,* Waveland Press, Inc. (1988). Print.

Guest, A.H., *Your Move: A New Approach to the Study of Movement and Dance,* Routledge. (1983). Print.

Sofras, P.A., *Dance Composition Basics: Capturing the Choreographer's Craft*, Human Kinetics. (2006). Print.

Choreographer Chapter Assessment

Submit a video or DVD of two original choreographies. One should be a solo choreography. The other should be for at least two people. If you submit a beginner piece, either show on paper or performance how you could change it to better suit more advanced students. If your piece is taught to intermediates, show me how you could simplify it for beginners. Please include choreography notes that include a map of the music and blocking. Be sure to point out the elements (repetition, mirroring, contrasting, etc.) that you used in your choreography. Explain why they were used. If you left certain things out, be sure to comment on why they were left out. Make sure that the entire choreography can be seen in the video. The dance should include:

- a beginning/entrance
- repetition
- variety
- balance
- consideration of the number of people in the dance
- consideration of the space where the dance will be performed
- a conclusion/exit

Your video/DVD should also show knowledge of all the previous material.

Include a self-critique with ideas on what you could have done differently to improve the pieces, as well as what you think you did well.

Remember: Don't be afraid to stretch yourself. Attempt something that you are unsure about. Don't be afraid of feedback. The more you challenge yourself in your assessment, the greater your potential to learn.

Choreography Chapter Assessment Results

Student name:_____ Date:_____

Items are scored on a 0-5 point scale. The goal is to achieve a 3, which means that you understand the material.

0- did not attempt
1- did not demonstrate a good understanding of the material
2- demonstrated some understanding of the material
3- demonstrated an understanding of the material
4- demonstrated good understanding of the material
5- demonstrated a mastery of the material

___ choreography suits the students' skill level
___ choreography suits the number of people in the piece
___ choreography follows the musical construction
___ choreography timing is appropriate
___ choreography spacing is appropriate
___ choreography energy is appropriate
___ choreography form is appropriate
___ map of music adequately reflects the music
___ music is blocked in a logical way that shows a relationship to the whole
___ notes accurately reflect what is going on in the choreography (repetition, contrast, etc.)
___ choreography changes from simple to complex, or vice versa
___ choreography is matched to the dancers' skill level

Comments:

10 IMPROVISATION

Goal: Students will understand how to create simple improvisational exercises that develop confidence in improvisational skill.

Objective:
Students will be able to teach improvisation as demonstrated by their ability to create effective improvisational exercises that develop students' knowledge in three different areas of dance.

Improvisation

Improvisation is the core of any folk dance. Remember, folk dance is a dance by the people for the people. Even when you are line dancing using specific steps in a specific order, you see the individual soloist improvising on the spot, and then rejoining the line.

So what is improvisation? Improvisation is the spontaneous expression of music, movement, speech, or any other form of emotion. It can be skilled or unskilled, short or long, sad or happy, beautiful or repulsive. If we are performing for the pleasure of others, the common goal for most would be to make it entertaining and skilled.

I notice that improvisation seems to come to some people innately, while others feel that it is the most difficult thing to do. So how do you teach someone to do what they feel when they have no idea what they feel? How do you develop someone's ability to express what they feel in a musical and aesthetically pleasing way? This chapter will explore that.

Improvisation is wonderful because it gives beginning level dancers the ability to perform or explore without having to learn a whole choreography. Professionals can be spontaneous and make each dance personal to the crowd that is viewing it. Students can explore elements of dance to gain a deeper understanding of the pieces. Using improvisation in class is a great way to keep classes varied, fun, and challenging.

This chapter was saved for last because good improvisation requires you to break down movement, understand musical structure, understand musicality, and work with the elements of choreography. Having already explored all those elements should make teaching improvisation easier. However, this does not mean that improvisation should be saved for those in higher levels. Improvisation can and should be practiced at every level.

Improvisation for Beginners

One of the biggest obstacles to improvising as a beginner is fear. I recall that if I had been asked to dance by myself where everyone else in the class could see me, I would have quit after the first class. There was no way I was going to do that! Not even if everyone else was doing something at the same time.

As a result, I think that tackling the fear of improvisation in a classroom setting is one of the first things a teacher should do. You do that by normalizing the experience, providing support, and letting the student decide how much she wants to participate.

For example, I ended my Foundations class with a five-minute free dance during which students could follow me or do their own thing. Everyone danced at the same time in class formation facing the mirror. I think this made it seem more like a continuation of class and less like improvisation.

I used the same song every class, so students had familiarity with the music. The music was moderately paced; therefore, everyone could keep up. It was also fairly simplistic, so no Turkish drops or wild spins were indicated.

I danced eight or sixteen counts of the same basic movement before switching to another one, so transitions were predictable. The movements reflected the sound quality of the music, so smooth sounds were paired with smooth moves. Students who were new or shy could follow me. Those who were more adventurous or more confident could do their own thing. There was a dry erase board with moves printed on it at the front of the class. As long as they could remember what movement went along with each word, students could use this as a crutch.

The normalization part of this plan comes from doing it in every class and having everyone participate. No one was singled out to perform by themselves. Everyone did the same thing. It was just what we did. No big deal.

The support part of this plan came from the option for some people to follow me. Nobody was left "out there" wondering what to do. Even if the student didn't want to follow me, there usually wasn't just one lone wolf dancing to her own drummer. The women who were confident and skilled enough to come up with their own moves often stood close to one another, creating support for each other.

Because each student had been given the ability to choose whether she wanted to follow me or do her own thing, they were each in control of how much they wanted to participate. If they wanted to switch back and forth between soloing and following, as many did as they started their exploration, that was fine, too.

So how does this teach improvisation? It doesn't really, but imitation provides a framework to get them ready to improvise. *Follow me* is not improvisation. *Follow me while I dance phrases that are musical* gives them ideas of what movements to pair with particular sounds. Even though I have not yet started breaking down musicality as a concept, most of them will pick this up by participating.

I never had anyone drop class or sit out because of this approach to improvisation (however, they could). There was no fear. In fact, it was the favorite part of every class. Once the improv song came on, some people actually cheered!

Improvisation for Beyond Basics

The Beyond Basics student knows the movements, what they are called, and can string a few things together as combinations. This level of student probably will need a bit more freedom and challenge than is provided in the previous exercise. For this level of student and for one-time introductory classes, I use the circle dance construct.

The circle dance starts by teaching four to five eight-count moves that are done in sequence in a circle formation. They are simple moves to execute and remember, but have some variety from each other. For example, the moves used might be a big stroke little stroke (travel), hip circle (smooth), head slide (percussive), and a shoulder shimmy (percussive travel) for four counts walking into the circle and four counts walking back. The point isn't to try to create something that is visually stunning. The point is to provide a framework (the circle) so that everyone can participate as a group, while also providing solo opportunities for the more adventurous students.

The music is repetitive, simple tribal or pop music that doesn't have any tricky stops or dramatic build-ups. Five minutes should be the maximum time limit.

The dance starts by everyone doing the moves in sequence. The last movement is the cue for the solo to begin. The soloist enters the center of the circle and does her own thing for four or five counts of eight, then exits on cue so that another soloist can enter. If more than one soloist volunteers at once, they share the time.

Normalizing occurs by doing this on a regular basis. This could be the finale of your beyond basics class. Support comes from the group that surrounds you. This can be created by normalizing cheering or zaghareeting for the student in the middle. You might be amazed at how affirming this is. Control comes from the ability to decide whether or not you want to go into the middle and what to do once you get there. You might decide to do it this week or eight weeks from now.

At this point, it doesn't matter if the soloist is doing something pretty or expressive. It just matters that she's stringing movements together in the moment. You may notice that she seems to be counting or trying to reproduce something she's practiced. Some people have to create structure to feel comfortable. That's okay if that's what it takes to get her out there, but encourage freedom and spontaneous expression. This exercise is not about showing off or planning a 32-count choreography. It's about experiencing the moment. If you model stage presence and personal expression, it may also entice them to experiment with that.

Improvisation for the Intermediate

Once students have a firm grasp of basic movements, can execute combinations and transitions smoothly, and have a beginning understanding of choreography, the fun begins. You can explore so many realms of improvisation that will enhance confidence, skill, and interest in their dances. Recall from chapter two that as the dancer's ability grows, the teacher should be dancing less and the student should be self-correcting more. Here is one area in which you can see that begin to happen.

Exploring Elements of Dance Through Improvisation

Time

Recall from chapter four that timing refers to how fast, slow, and long-lasting a movement is. Timing also refers to how movements are phrased and accented. You can explore time with a metronome, repeating drum rhythm, or music.

When starting something new, it's a good idea to start with structure, and then move towards chaos. One exercise to explore time is to start with a repeating Beledi rhythm. Have students follow you, moving only on the one, two, three, and four. Once they have the hang of that, instruct them to choose their own movements but keep the same pace. Collect observations. Now have them follow you moving on the one, and, two, and, three, and, four, and counts. Once they have the hang of that, allow them to choose their own movements, keeping the same pace. Collect observations. Now have them dance at different speeds within the four-count phrase (Beledi is a four-count rhythm), doing some fast, moderate, and slow. Notice that the class is not interpreting things musically. They are simply improvising to timing. While this is not musical, exercises like this contribute to their understanding of the importance of timing and can strengthen their musicality, because it can take them out of dancing to the beat and put them in a place of dancing *with* the beat.

Here is another exercise for working with timing:

Start with a four or eight count phrase. Accent the one with a percussive movement. Then accent the one with a smooth movement. Then accent the three. The counts can vary in time. For example, while the accent may start on the one, the count of the accent may last for a whole count or several. Guide students through this process, then let them play with it on their own. Allow half the class to watch and then share observations. Switch places, allowing those who watched to dance and those who danced to watch. Share observations on what was seen as well as felt. Keeping those observations in mind, repeat the exercise and note the differences in expression this time.

Here is one of my favorite exercises for working with timing that can be adjusted to focus on many different aspects of dynamics changes. Start with a dry-erase board with four basic movements listed on it. The instructor demonstrates how to do each movement for eight counts each. Then the instructor does the same movement for eight counts each, but with variations. For example, if the first movement is a figure eight, she might do it the first time using two counts per side, then do it the second time using four counts of eight per side (in other words, twice as slowly the second time). If the next move is a hip circle, she might do it very big and slow the first time, then twice as fast the second time. Allow the class to improvise, using just these four movements. For example, if your four movements were: hip circle, 3-point turn, undulation, and shimmy, students would perform each of those movements for eight counts before moving to the next one, and then repeating the cycle again. Each time the cycle repeats, the timing of the movements would be different.

Space

Working with space gives lots of variety in dance composition. There is the space above you, below you, around you, and between you and another person. Space can be covered in a straight line, circle, spiral, zigzag, square, or in a random fashion. The concept of space changes as the dancer approaches the audience, withdraws, or turns her back. Space also sends psychological messages if we stand in one place or cover lots of ground.

Exploring use of space through improvisation can help your students tremendously expand their understanding of artistry.

Exercise One:

Divide the class into dancers and observers. Have the dancers spread out in the room. Count off so that each dancer is either a one or a two. Have the ones start by doing traveling steps, while the twos do stationary moves. When the instructor calls out, "change," the ones switch to stationary moves, while the twos change to traveling steps. Give the groups about 30 seconds each to play with the different movements before changing. Continue for about three minutes. Allow for creativity and fun. Ask for observations from participants and observers at the end of the exercise. Switch so that observers become dancers and dancers become participants and repeat.

This exercise tends to be a good learning tool for dancers who either use too much space or not enough. It can help balance the flow of traveling movement vs. stationary movement. It can build awareness of the psychology of staging. It can create an awareness of high space vs. low space. Observation is a powerful tool. Dancers can learn a lot by watching, so make sure to build in opportunities to watch others.

Exercise Two:

Split into two groups—observers and dancers. Have the dancers count off into two groups. The ones will travel in curved or circular patterns with soft turns and spins. The twos will travel in linear patterns with angular, right angle turns, and spins. Dancers can travel, turn, spin, or stop randomly. When the instructor says, "go," the dancers must move around each other. Do this for about three minutes, and then ask for observations. Once you have feedback, allow the observers to dance and dancers to observe.

This exercise can help dancers gain an awareness of spacing in group formations, floor patterns, and directional spacing (where is the audience and the impact of this facing on the audience). It may also help them to see the impact of curves vs. lines while dancing, and give them an idea of where one might be more desirable than other in certain places.

Energy

Have you ever seen two dancers perform the same choreography with the same skill level and get very different audience reactions? This is probably due to the energy that each dancer conveyed. Energy refers to the quality of movement. Some dancers are very busy and fast, but have a frenetic quality about them, while others can dance with the same speed, but leave the audience feeling alive and excited. Some dancers do a slow taxim that is about exciting as watching paint dry, while another can dance to the same music at the same speed and have everyone riveted to their seat. Don't confuse energy with speed, tension, or intensity. It's more like the ability to capture and convey a feeling of something like floating, collapsing, suspension, or sharpness.

Exercise One:

Have dancers form two lines. Dancers are to dance across the floor gaining energy as they go, so they approach the far side of the room energy builds. As they come back, energy contracts. As the dancer in front of them reaches the halfway mark across the floor, the dancer behind her follows. Once the entire line has crossed the floor, the first dancer starts again from a place of high intensity to a place of low intensity. Dancers should be present as they are dancing, but watching as they are standing in line. If this is too distracting, split them into two groups so that one watches as the other performs. Ask for observations after the fact.

This exercise should build awareness of how energy feels in the body and is interpreted by the audience. It should help them to spot places in their dance where their energy could be changed for maximum impact or should be reduced because it's too intense.

Exercise Two:

The instructor writes qualities of energy on a dry erase board such as changes in intensity (hard, soft), quality (floating, sticky, lethargic), and accent (off beat, on beat, rhythmically). She instructs students to use these different qualities of energy when the music calls for them. (This should be a familiar piece of music). Students share observations of what that was like. A variation could be to dance against the music. This can often open up creative possibilities.

This exercise should build awareness of musicality and open up ways of expressing themselves.

Form

Form is what gives dance structure. It is generally created by the form given by the music. Music doesn't rigidly lay out a map, but it will tell you where to put the smooth, percussive, and travel sections of your dance.

Exercise One:

Have two dancers volunteer to be the demonstrators. One will do a move or combination of about eight counts or so, while the other follows with specific instructions to change the interpretation of what the leader is doing. For example, if the leader does a hip drop and the follower is instructed to mirror her, she will imitate in such a way that is identical when facing the leader. The class has to guess which form element is being used and give feedback on what they see. Once they have done that, select a new leader and follower to demonstrate.

Some elements of form that you can experiment with are asymmetry (deliberately creating imbalance for a specific effect), quality (same movement with a different feeling), repetition, retrograde (performing the movement backward), alternating the accent, changing the speed, using a different part of the stage, and symmetry.

This exercise can help build an awareness of the elements of form so that dancers can start working with them. The feedback can give them ideas of what may work within their own repertoire.

Exercise Two:

Dancers pair up. One is the leader and the other is the follower. The leader repeats a simple 8 or 16-count combination, while the follower either does the same thing in an exaggerated way or does the same thing in an opposite, understated way. For example, if the leader does a middle of the road hip circle followed by a hip drop, the follower can do an extremely big hip circle with a rough hip drop. If the leader does a smooth ami followed by a dainty chest drop, the follower can do a jerky ami followed by a heavy chest drop.

This exercise can get dancers playing with contrasting moods that they may not have considered before. It can get them outside of their comfort zone to expand creativity.

Putting It All Together

Working with the elements of dance in a creative, off the cuff manner gives you freedom to be absurd, innovative, or amusing. It encourages you to let out your inner clown, temptress, and sorrow. It gives you a container to explore emotions, so that dance is more than just mechanical exercises. It allows you to be you in small, safe doses. As your knowledge grows, you may not have to think about what place on the stage will get the most impact for a particular move. You will just know and be there when you need to be. Your confidence will grow because doing things spontaneously will have been rehearsed over and over again.

Improvisation is really hard for some people and is challenging for most people to do well. There are just so many possibilities. By focusing on elements of dance, you chunk improvisation down to bite-sized pieces. It's a LOT easier to say to the class, "I want you to dance for three minutes using only shimmies," than to say, "Okay, I am going to put on some music and I want you to improvise for three minutes." Once they are good at playing with space, then you can add another element and another until one day you can say, "Dance to this music for three minutes," and not only can everyone do it without freezing, thinking, or freaking out, but it actually looks pretty good, too.

If you have mastered music theory, rhythms, musicality, and choreography, you have all the elements you need to do improvised performance. Improvisation is not just the ability to dance on the fly. Good improvisation is the art of combining all the elements of dance spontaneously, effectively, and skillfully.

Resources for Further Study

Books

Green Gilbert, A. *Creative Dance for All Ages: A Conceptual Approach.*, Amer Alliance for Health Physical. (1992). Print.

Morganroth, J., *Dance Improvisations.*, University of Pittsburgh Press. (1987). Print.

Improvisation Chapter Assessment

Submit a lesson plan outlining three original improvisational exercises, and then conduct them with a class. Include the goal and/or objectives of each exercise, observations on how well the material was absorbed, and observations on what could be improved upon. Submit a video or DVD of your students running through these exercises. Be sure to point out the elements (repetition, mirroring, contrasting, etc.) that you were illustrating.

Your video/DVD should also show knowledge of all the previous material.

Include a self-critique with ideas on what you could have done differently to improve the pieces, as well as what you think you did well.

Remember: I am not expecting perfection. Don't be afraid to stretch yourself. Attempt something that you are unsure about. Don't be afraid of feedback. The more you challenge yourself in your assessment, the greater your potential to learn.

Improvisation Chapter Assessment Results

Student name:_____   Date:_____

Items are scored on a 0-5 point scale. The goal is to achieve a 3, which means that you understand the material.

0- did not attempt
1- did not demonstrate a good understanding of the material
2- demonstrated some understanding of the material
3- demonstrated an understanding of the material
4- demonstrated good understanding of the material
5- demonstrated a mastery of the material

___ goal and/or objectives for exercise #1 was met
___ goal and/or objective for exercise #2 was met
___ goal and/or objective for exercise #3 was met
___ elements of dance were clearly identifiable in the exercises
___ exercises increased the student's ability to improvise well

Comments: (May include observations on all previous chapters). If goal and objectives were not met, full credit could be obtained by explaining why that happened and what changes could be made to make it more likely.

ABOUT THE AUTHOR

Taaj is an award-winning dancer, teacher, and troupe director who has performed in Egypt and taught across the United States. Taaj is co-creator of the international dance publication, *Zaghareet!* Her articles have also been published in every major print and online belly dance magazine.

Taaj began teaching seriously in 2001. From 2002 to 2007, her students won forty-six trophies from competitions in four states. Taaj took what she learned from coaching those students and turned it into *The Belly Dance Trainer Method* so that others could benefit from her champion producing strategies.

www.ingramcontent.com/pod-product-compliance
Lightning Source LLC
Chambersburg PA
CBHW082042230426
43670CB00016B/2752